LITTLE CRIT

BEGINNING MATH

Preschool

Table of Contents

Columbus, Ohio

BEGINNING MATH

Preschool

Credits:
School Specialty Publishing Editorial/Production Team
Vincent F. Douglas, B.S. and M. Ed.
Tracey E. Dils
Janet D. Sweet
Jennifer Blashkiw Pawley
Amy Mayr

Big Tuna Trading Company Art/Editorial/Production Team
Mercer Mayer
John R. Sansevere
Erica Farber
Brian MacMullen
Matthew Rossetti
Kamoon Song
Soojung Yoo

A Big Tuna Trading Company, LLC/J.R. Sansevere Book

Send all inquiries to: School Specialty Publishing, 8720 Orion Place, Columbus OH 43240-2111

ISBN 0-7696-5149-6

2 3 4 5 6 7 8 9 10 WAL 10 09 08 07

WELCOME TO CRITTERVILLE!
Spider
Frog
Grasshopper
Mouse
Little Critter
Little Sister
Dad
Kitty
Mom
Blue
Gator
Bat Child
Gabby
Bun Bun
Tiger
Maurice
Molly
Malcolm

Big

Name ______________________________

Directions: Look at the pictures in each box. Circle the pictures that are **big.**

Small

Name

Directions: Look at the pictures in each box. Circle the pictures that are **small.**

Smallest to Biggest

Name ______________________

Directions: Have an adult cut out the boxes above. Then, on another sheet of paper, line up Little Critter's pets in order from **smallest** to **biggest**.

This page is blank for the
cutting activity on the opposite side
of the page.

Long

Name

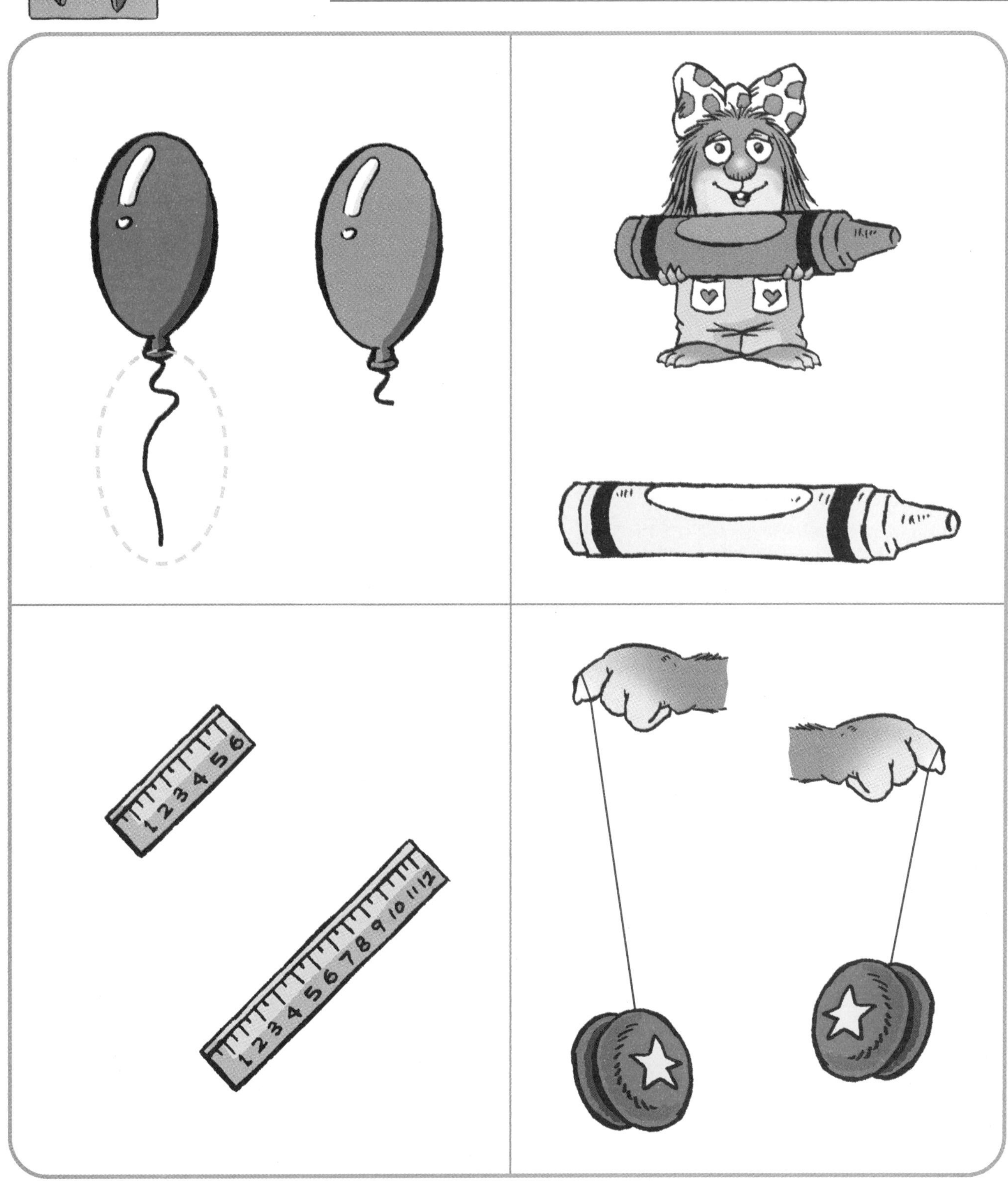

Directions: Look at the pictures in each box. Circle the objects that are **long.**

Short

Name

Directions: Look at the pictures in each box. Circle the pictures that are **short.**

Tall

Name ____________________

Directions: Look at the pictures in each box. Circle the pictures that are **tall.**

Full

Name

Directions: Look at the pictures in each box. Circle the containers that are **full.**

Empty

Name ____________________

Directions: Look at the pictures in each box. Circle the containers that are **empty.**

Circle

Name

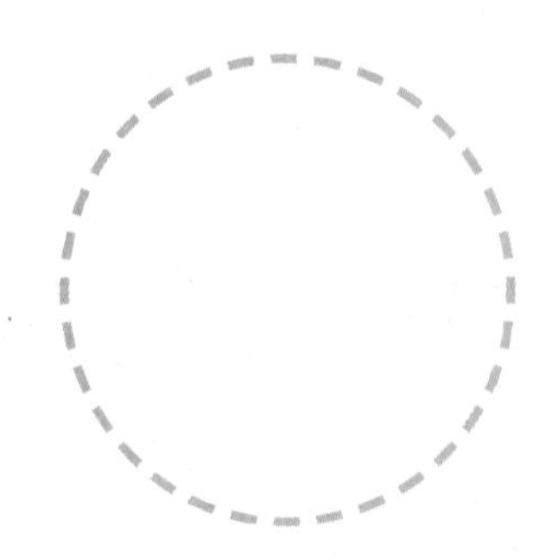

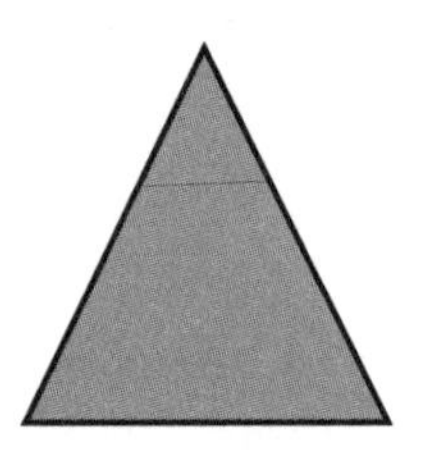

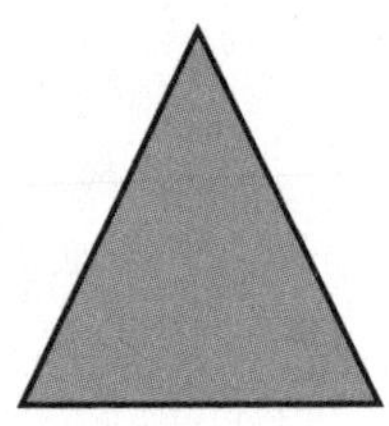
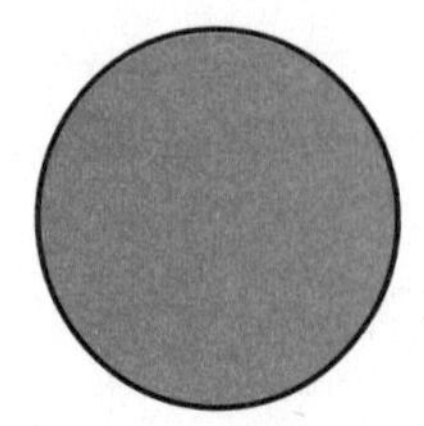

Directions: Trace the **circle** in the first row. Then draw a line under the circle in each row.

Find the Circles

Name

Directions: Tiger is fast asleep. Look at the objects in his room. Draw an **X** on each object that has the shape of a **circle.**

Square

Name

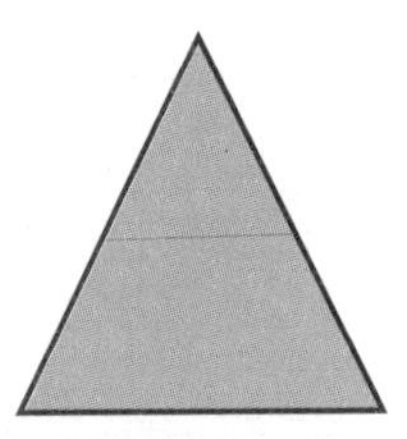

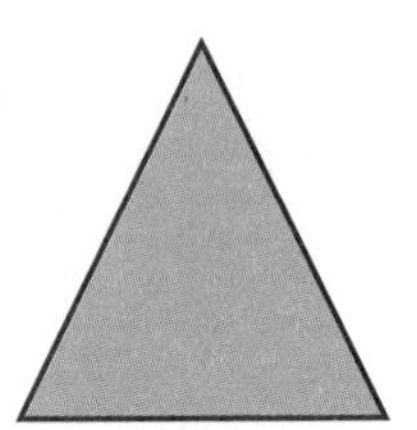

Directions: Trace the **square** in the first row. Then draw a line under the square in each row.

Find the Squares

Name ______________________

Directions: Gator and Bat Child are having a snack. Look at the objects in Gator's room. Draw an **X** on each object that has the shape of a **square.**

Triangle

Name

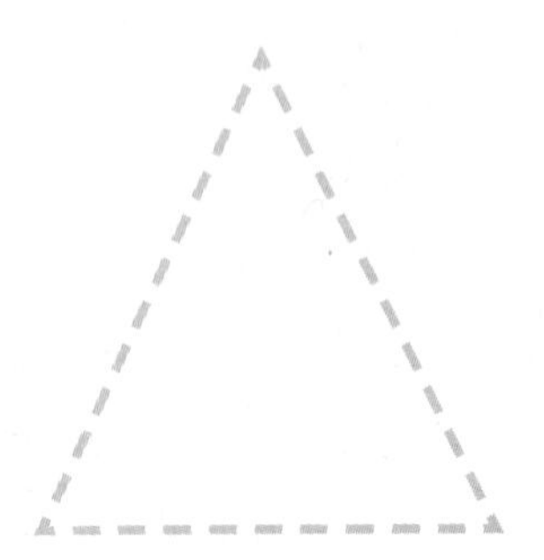

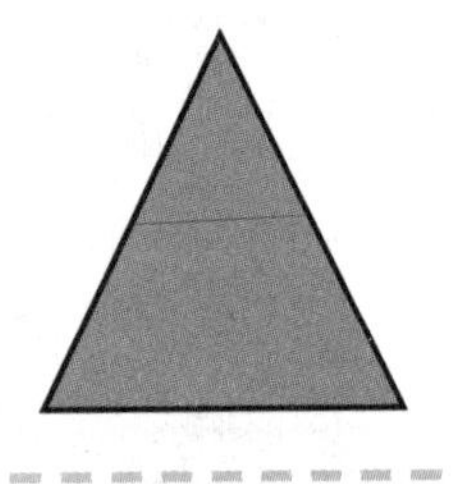

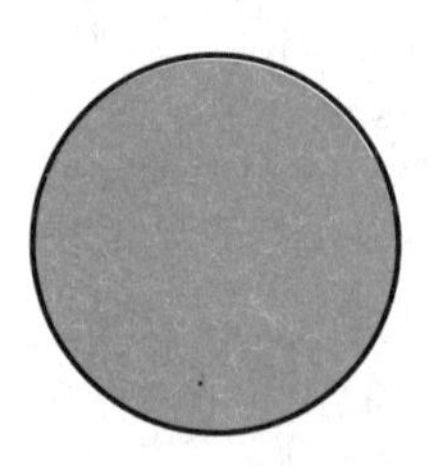

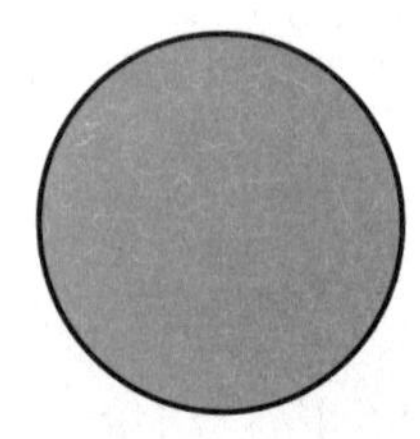

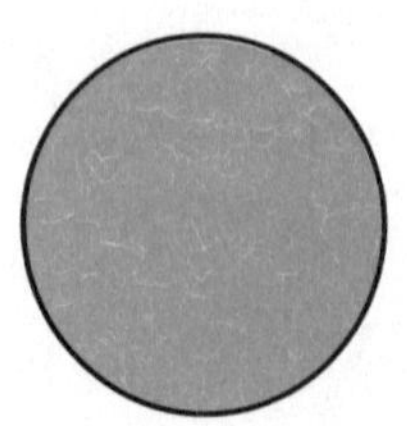

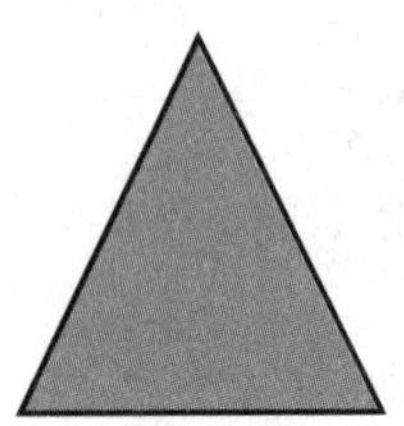

Directions: Trace the **triangle** in the first row. Then draw a line under the triangle in each row.

Find the Triangles

Name

Directions: Malcolm is camping. Look at Malcolm's campsite. Draw an **X** on each object that has the shape of a **triangle**.

Shapes: Review

Name ______________________

Directions: Look at the shapes in the picture. • Color the **circles** blue. • Color the **squares** red. • Color the **triangles** green.

Finish the Shapes

Name ______________________

Directions: Trace the dotted lines to complete the shape in each row. Then draw that shape at the end of each row.

Rectangle

Name

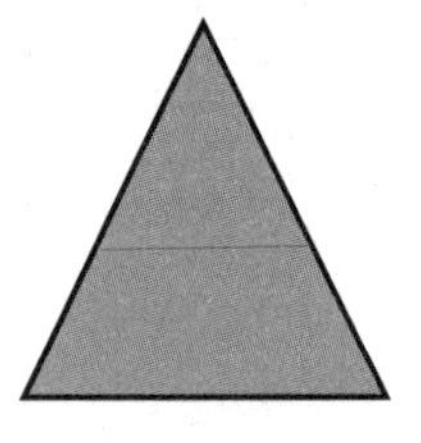

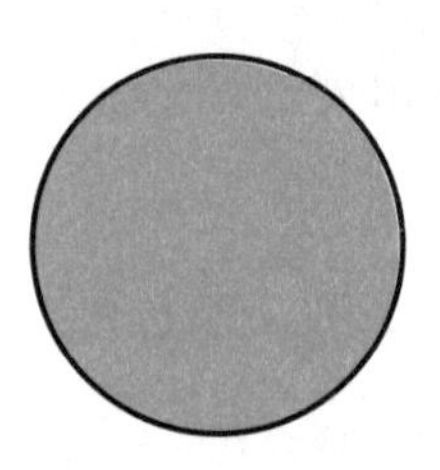

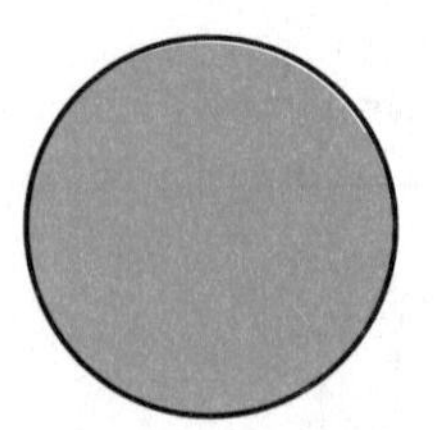

Directions: Trace the **rectangle** in the first row. Then draw a line under the rectangle in each row.

Finding the Rectangles

Name

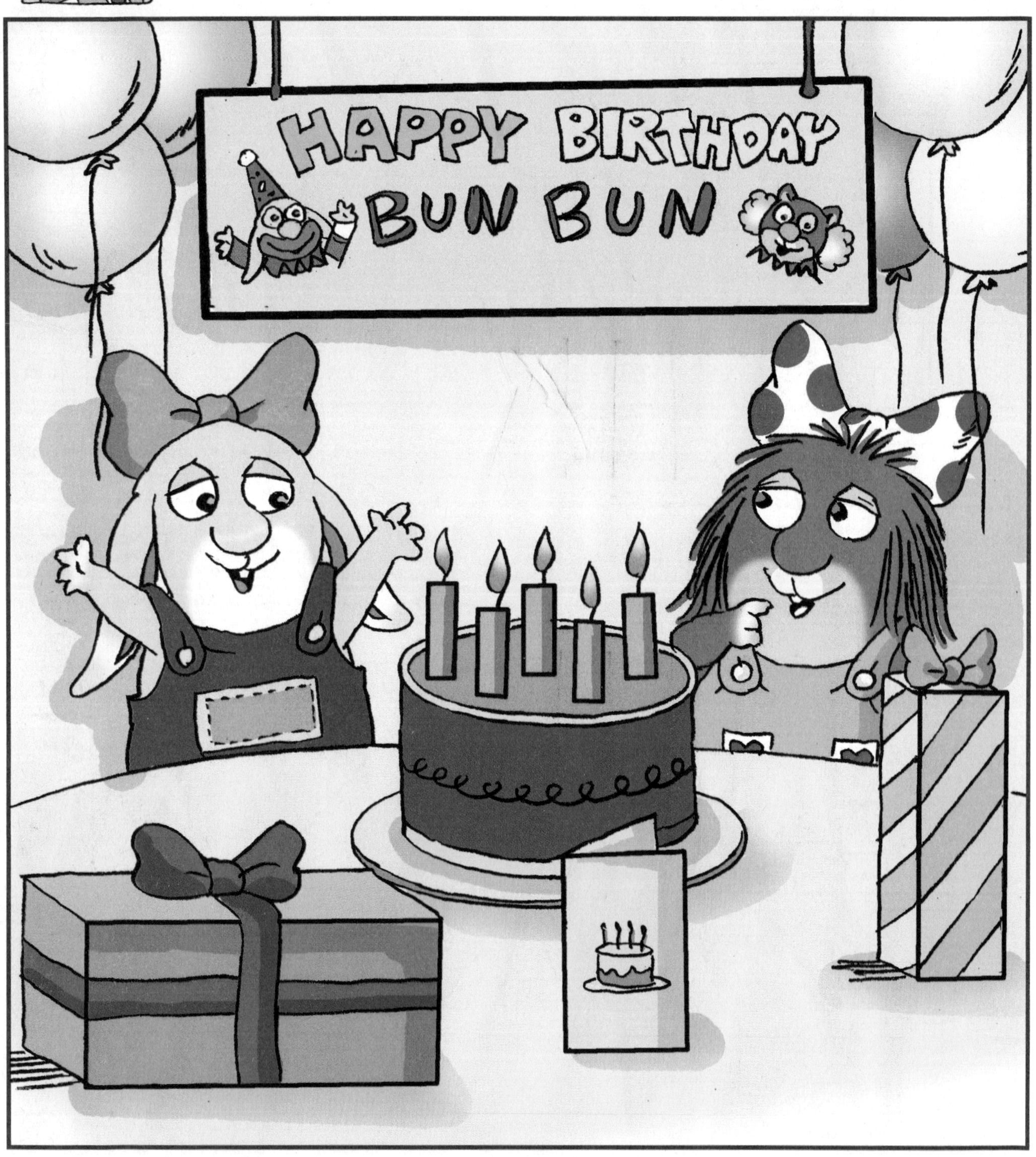

Directions: It's Bun Bun's birthday. Look at the objects at her party. Draw an **X** on each object that has the shape of a **rectangle.**

Shapes: Review

Name ______________________________

Directions: Little Critter is taking a bath. Look at the objects in the picture. •Color the **circle.** •Draw a line from the **rectangle** to Little Critter. •Draw an **X** on the **squares.** •Draw a line under the **triangle.**

Shape Art

Name ______________________________

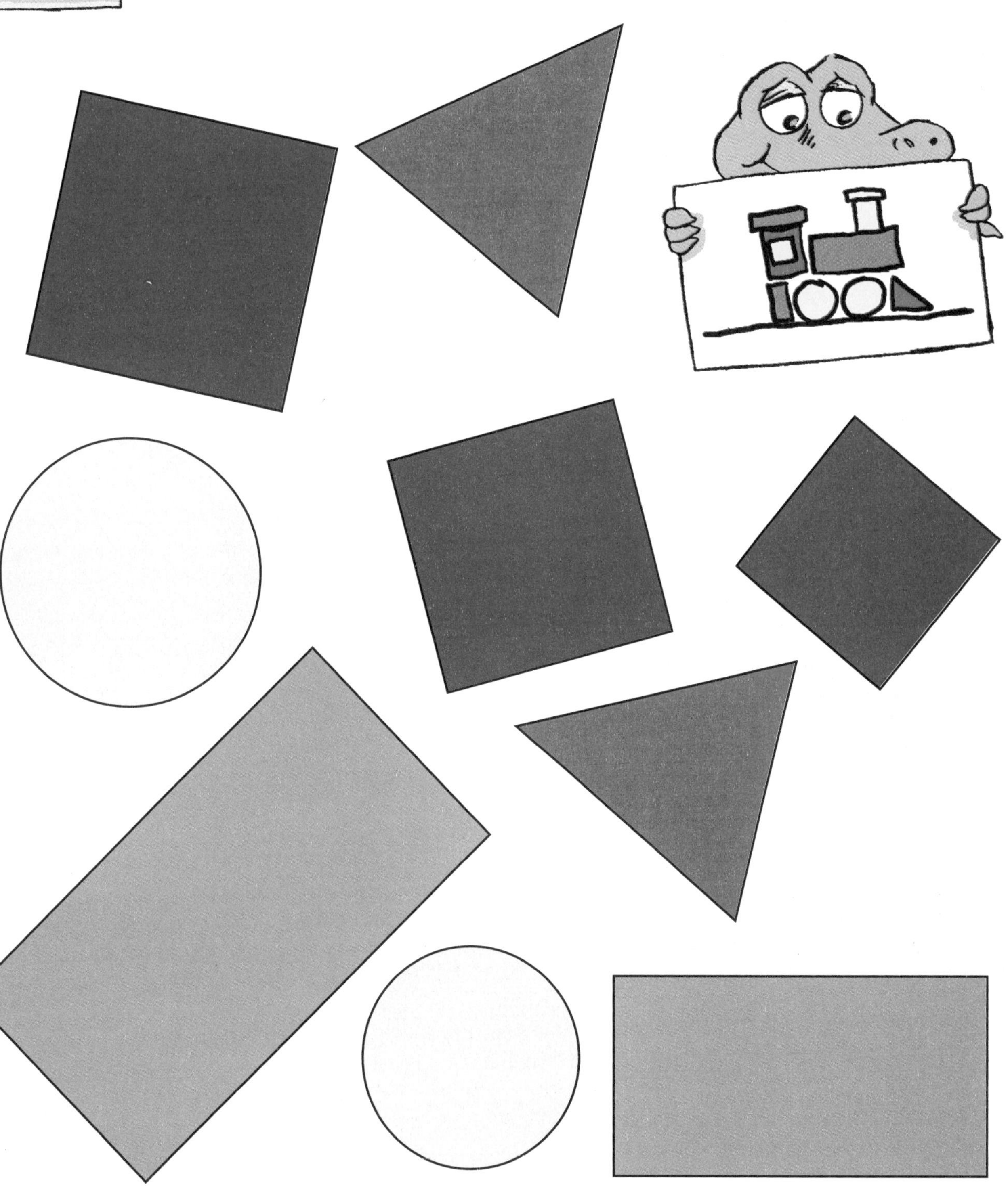

Directions: Have an adult cut out the shapes above. Then, glue the shapes on another sheet of paper to make a picture or design.

This page is blank for the cutting activity on the opposite side of the page.

Shapes: Review

Name

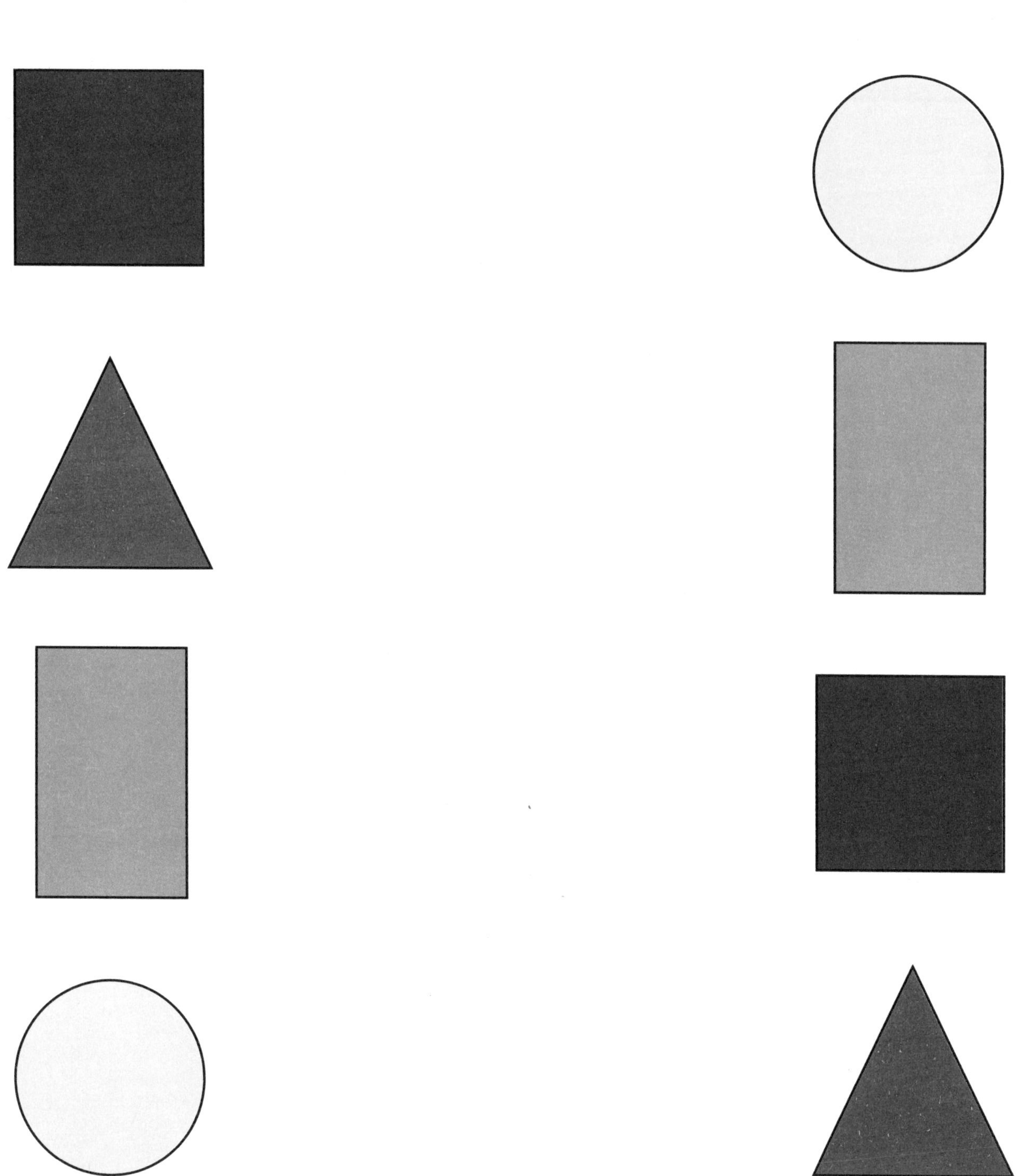

Directions: Draw a line to the matching shapes.

Oval

Name

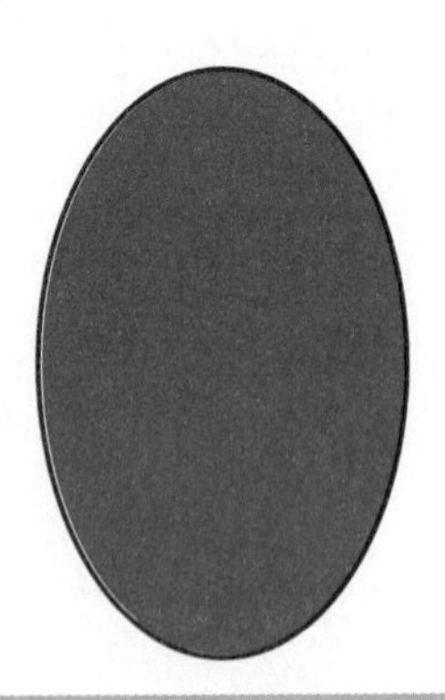

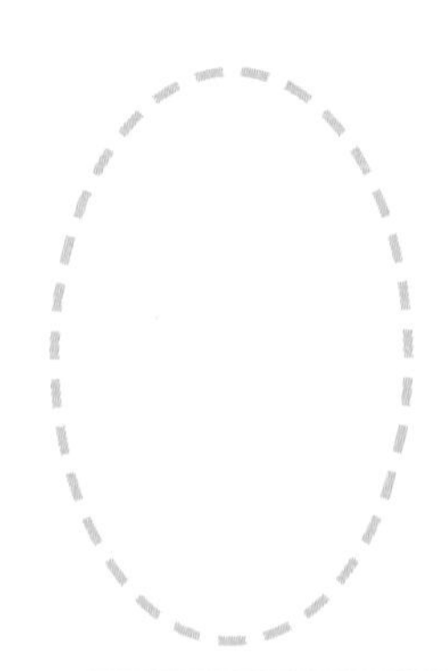

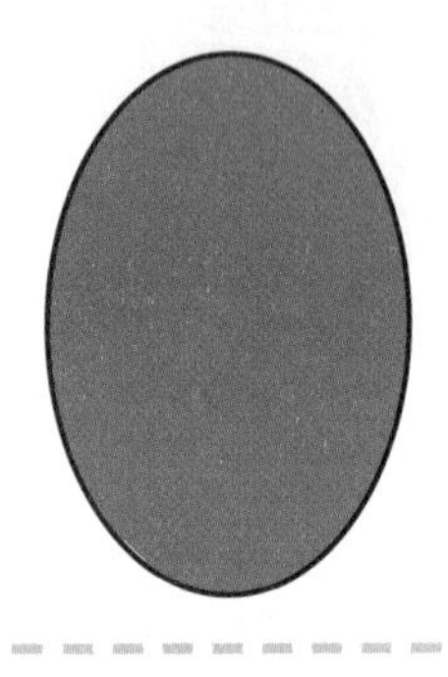

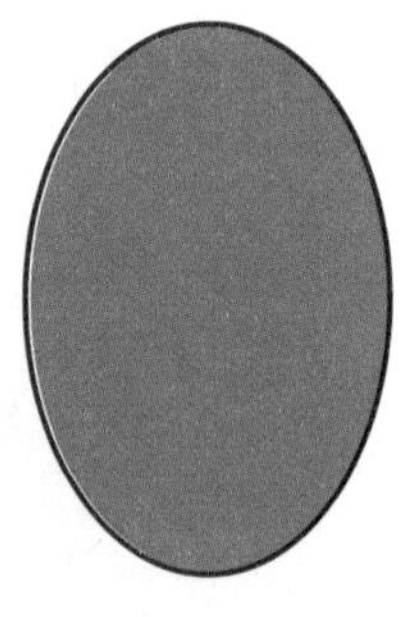

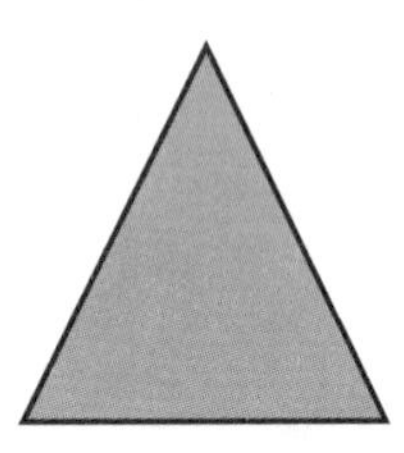

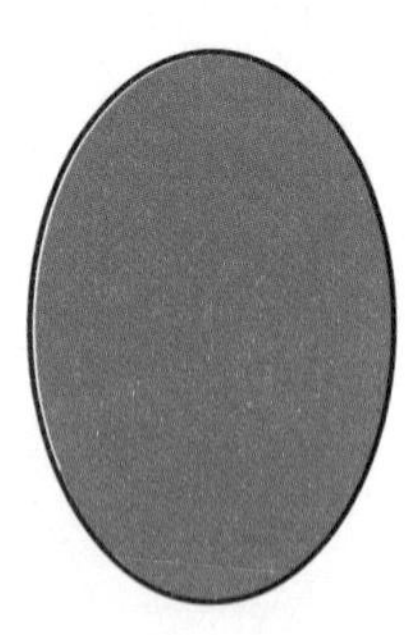

Directions: Trace the **oval** in the first row. Then draw a line under the oval in each row.

Find the Ovals

Name ______________________________

Directions: Little Sister is in the backyard. Look at the objects around her. Draw an **X** on each object that has the shape of an **oval.**

Star

Name

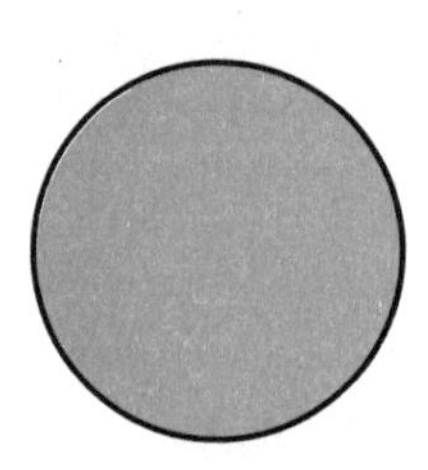

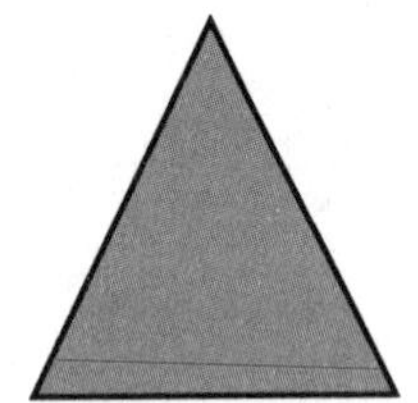

Directions: Trace the **star** in the first row. Then draw a line under the star in each row.

Find the Stars

Name

Directions: Maurice is looking for **stars.** Help him find them. Color all the stars blue.

Heart

Name

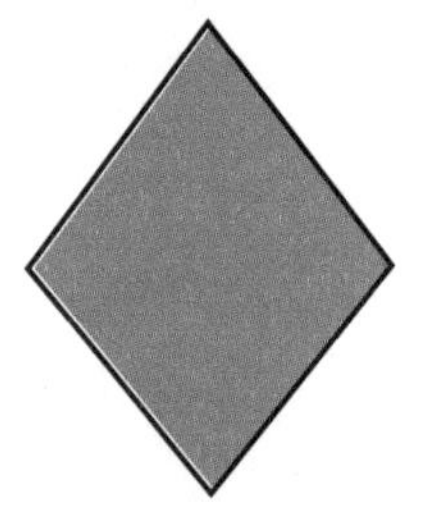

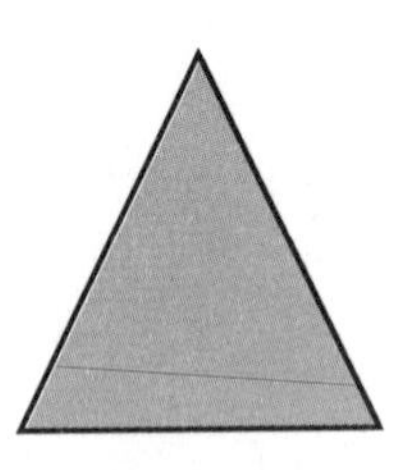

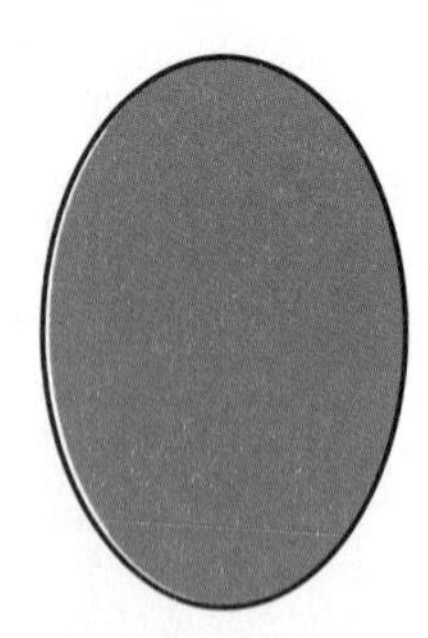

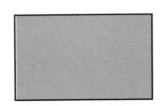

Directions: Trace the **heart** in the first row. Then draw a line under the heart in each row.

Find the Hearts

Name ______________________________

Directions: It's Valentine's Day in Critterville. Draw an **X** on each **heart** in the picture above.

Diamond

Name

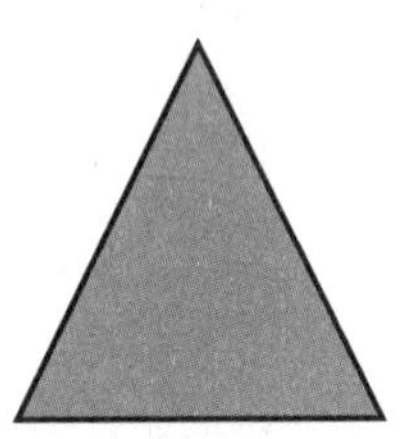

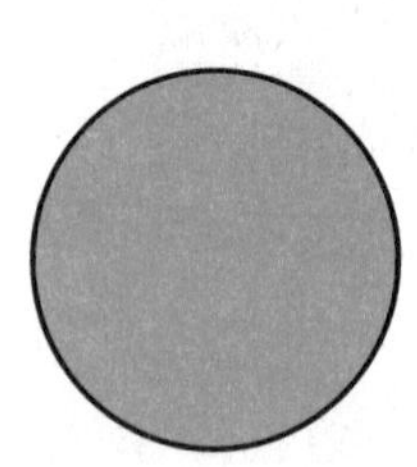

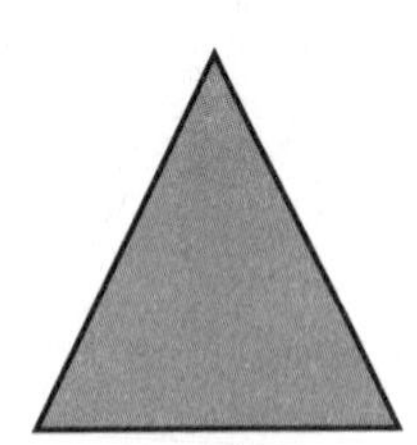

Directions: Trace the **diamond** in the first row. Then draw a line under the diamond in each row.

Find the Diamonds

Name ______________________________

Directions: Maurice, Molly, and Bun Bun are flying kites. Draw an **X** on each object that has the shape of a **diamond.**

Shapes: Review

Name

Color the **circles** red. 

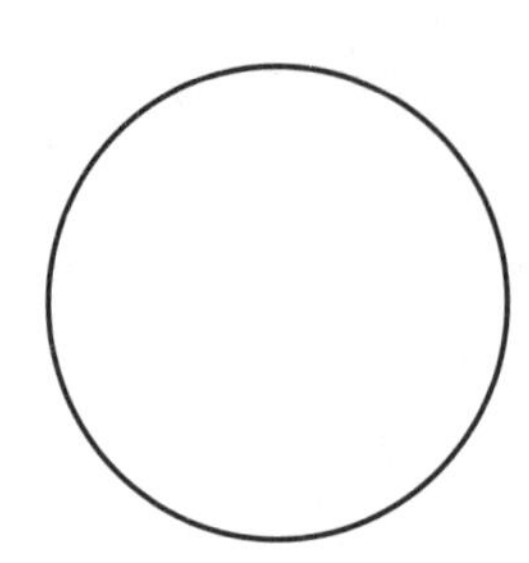 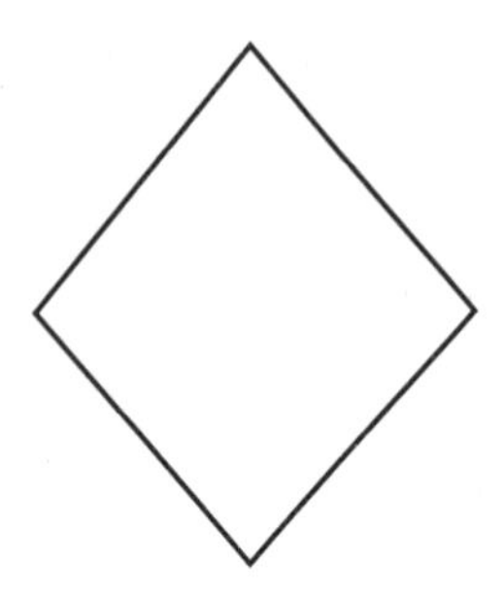 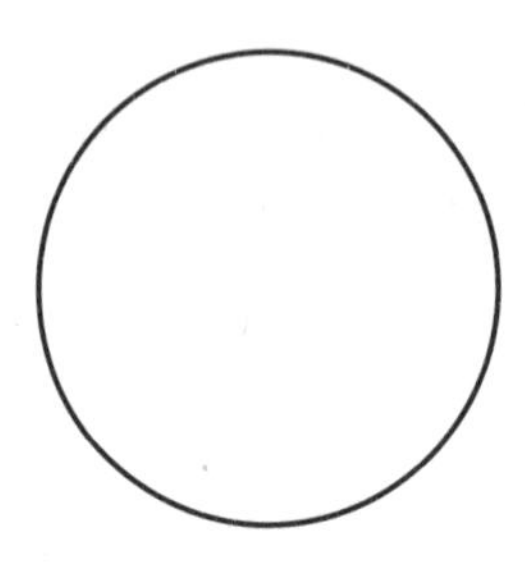 

Color the **rectangles** green. 

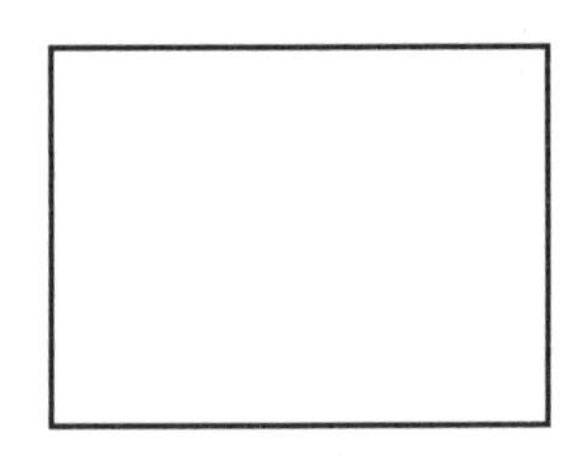   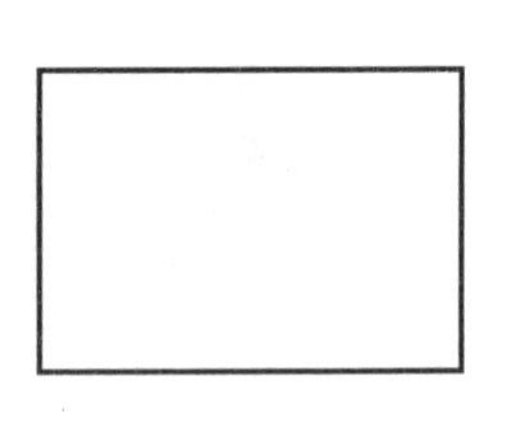

Color the **triangles** purple. 

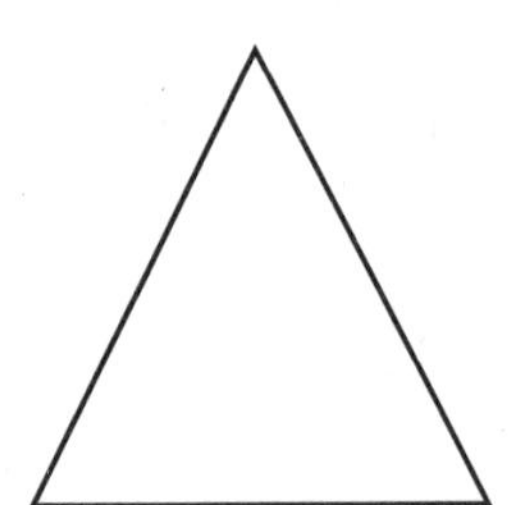 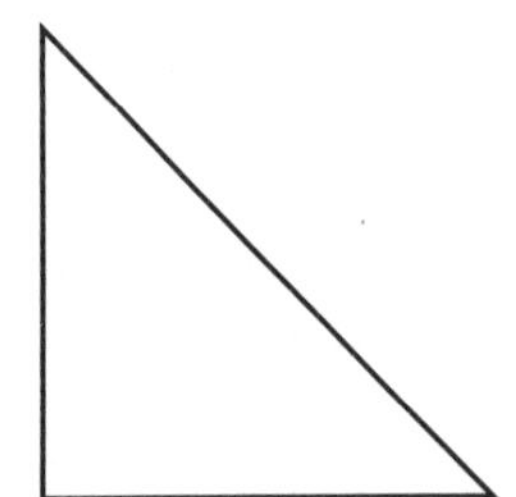 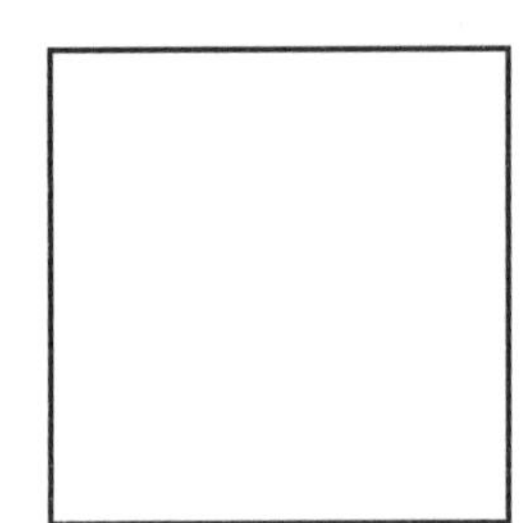 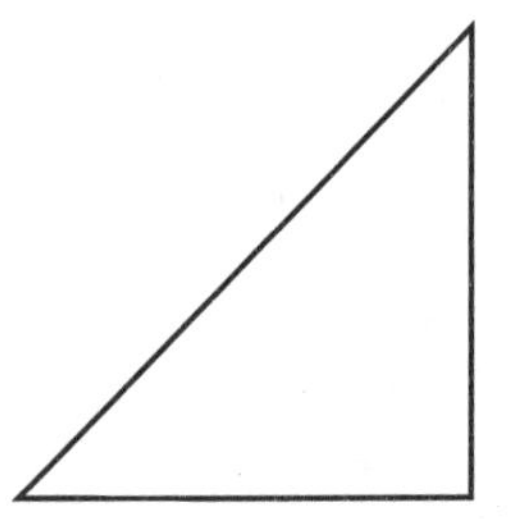

Follow the directions in each row above.

Shapes: Review

Name

Color the **squares** purple. 

 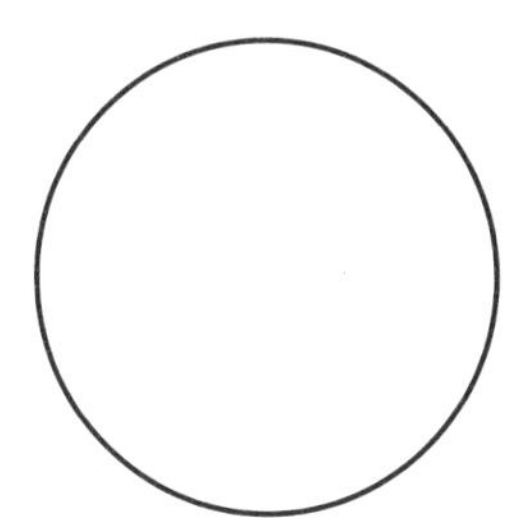 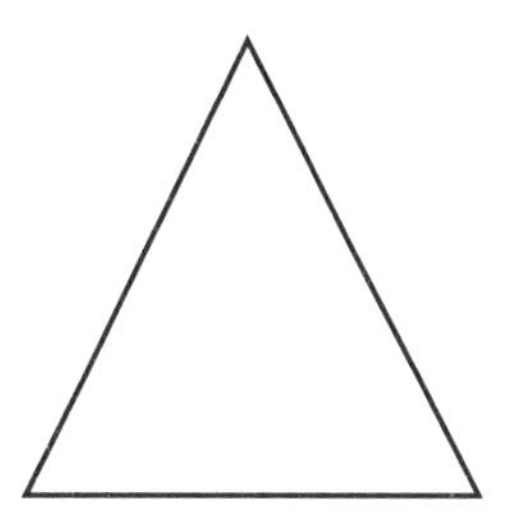 

Color the **hearts** blue. 

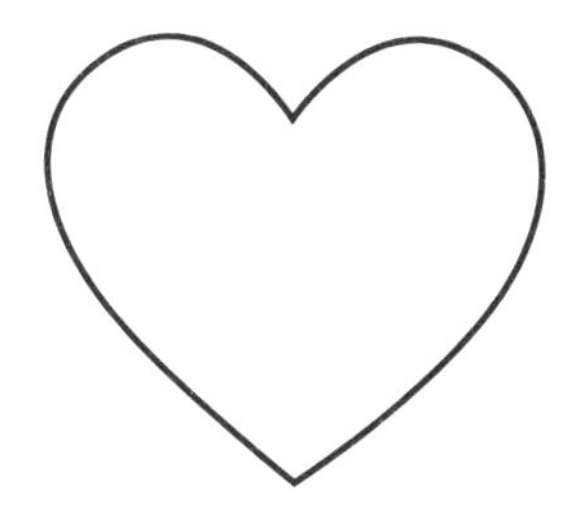 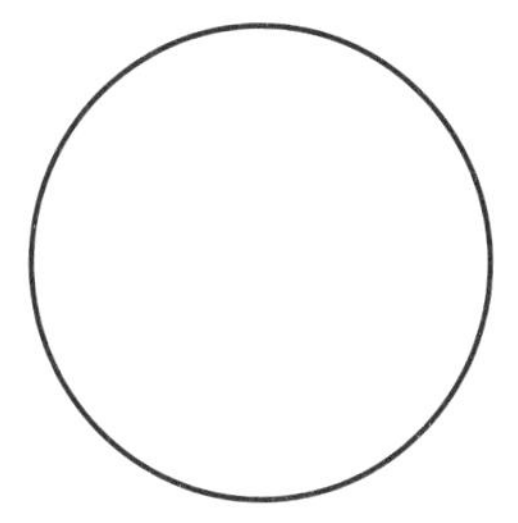 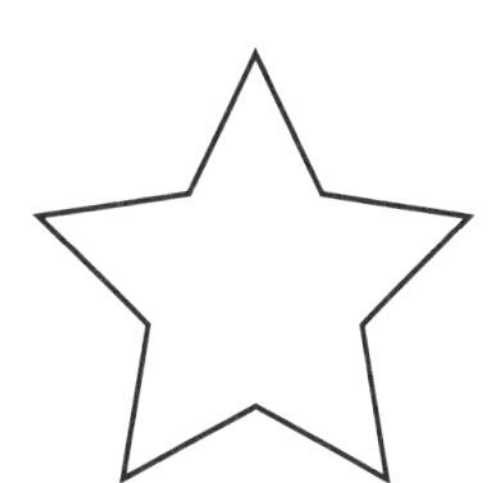 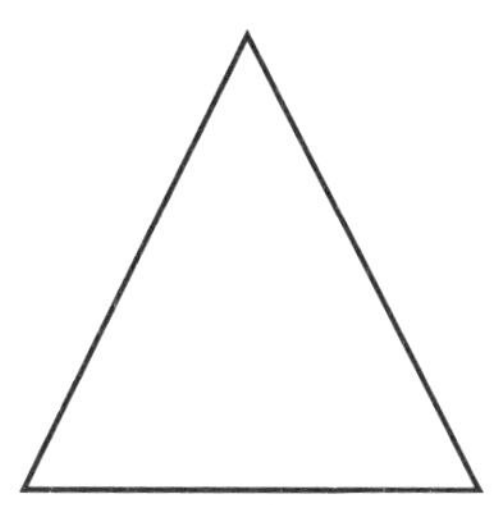

Color the **diamonds** yellow.

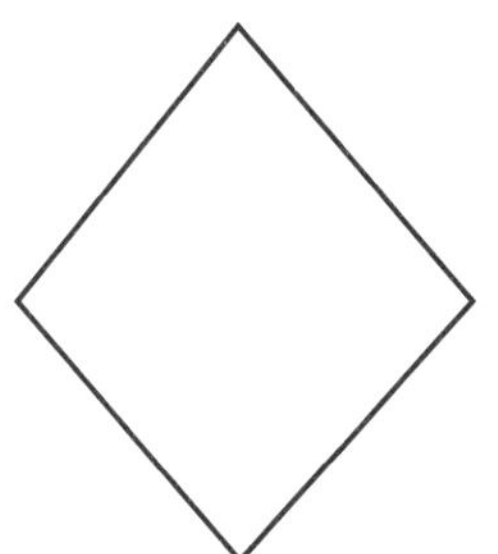  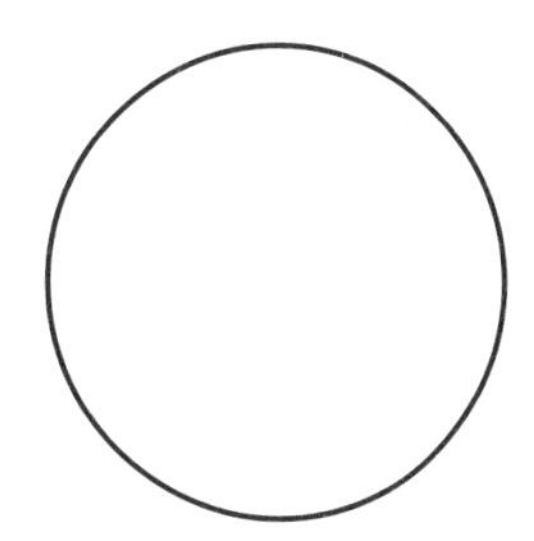 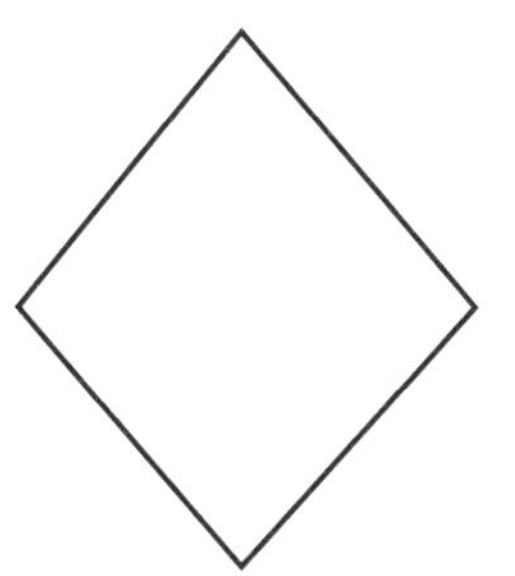

Follow the directions in each row above.

Patterns: Colors

Name

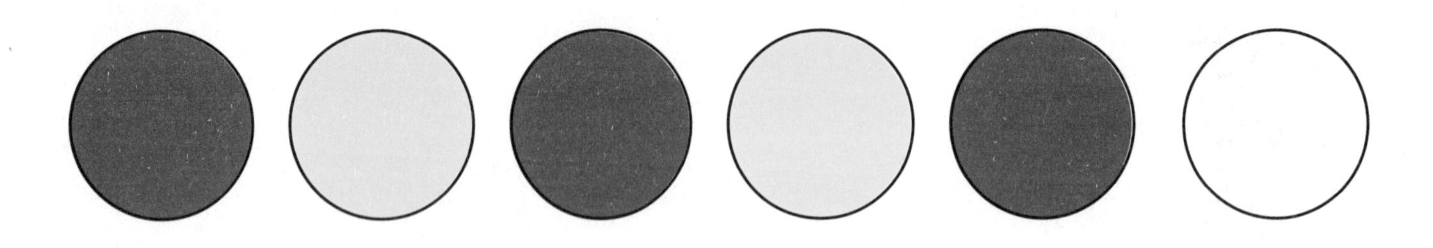

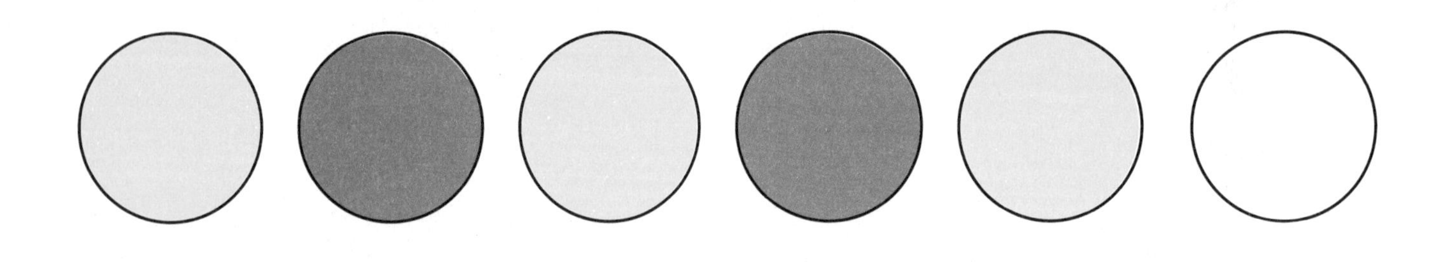

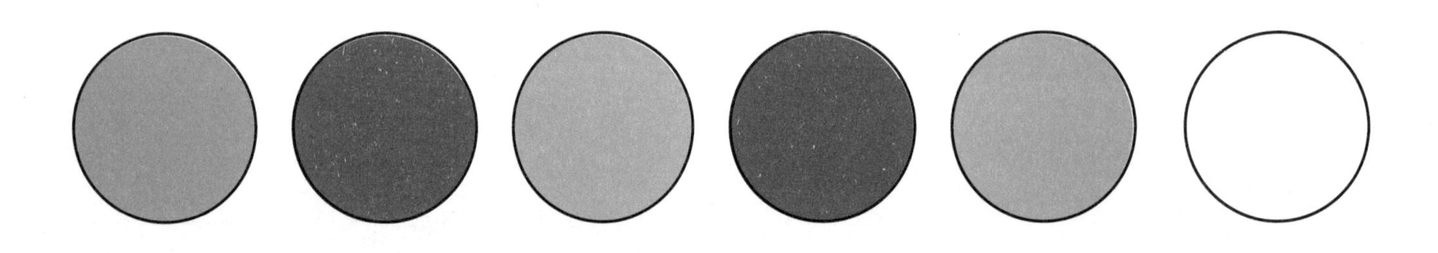

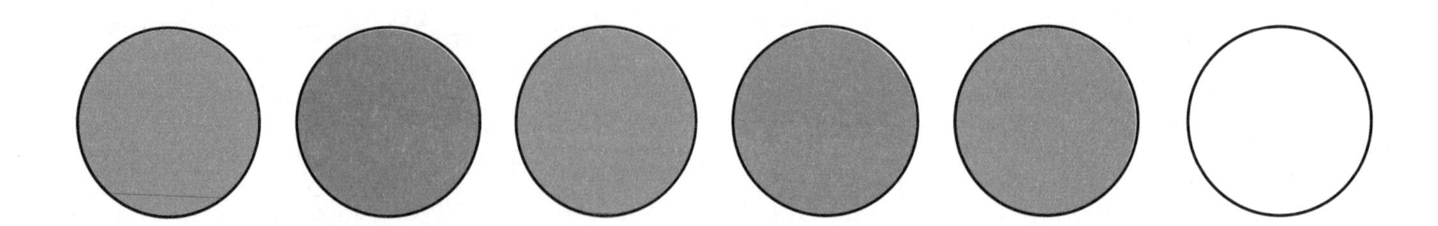

Directions: Fill in each circle with the color that comes next in each pattern.

Patterns: Colors

Name ______________________________

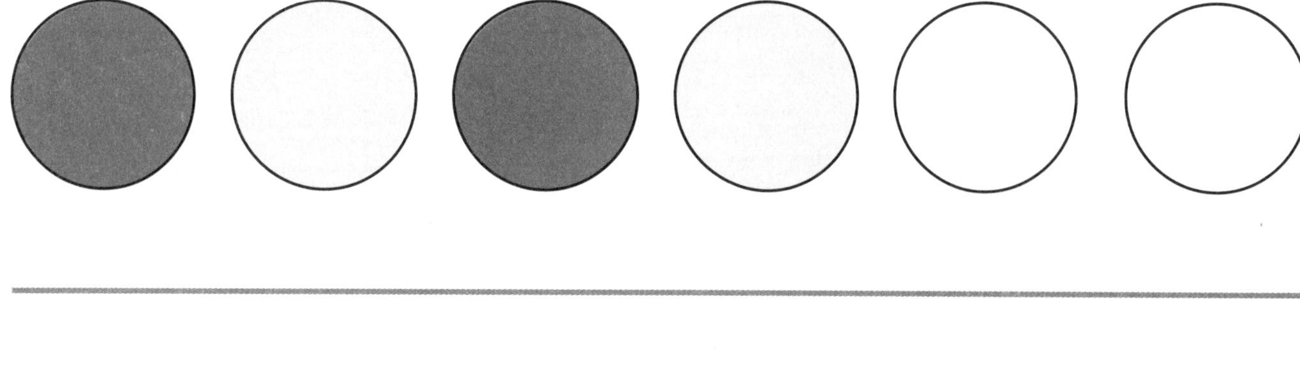

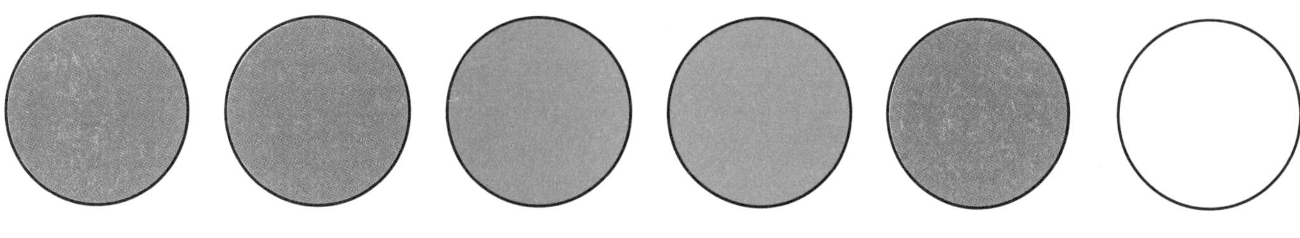

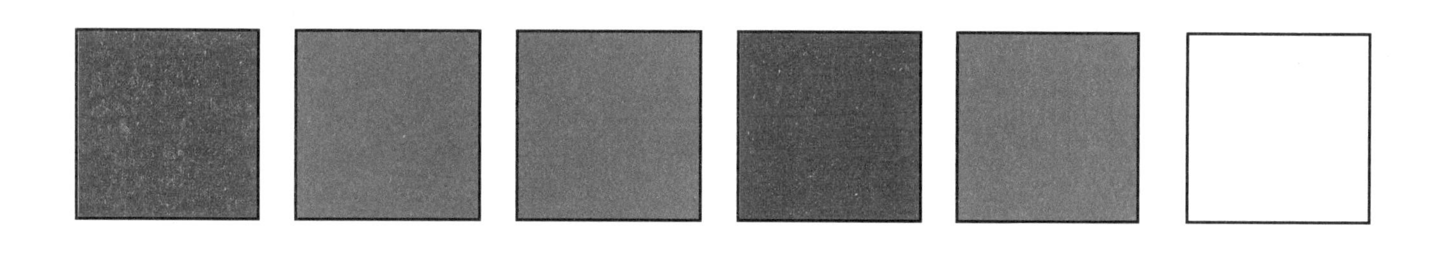

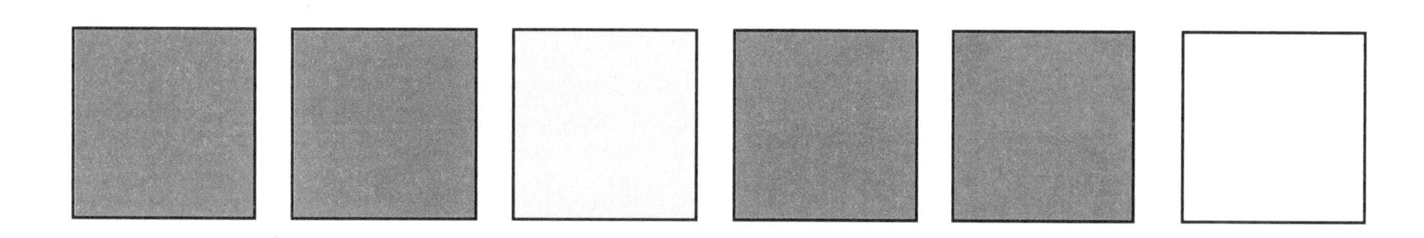

Directions: Fill in each shape with the color that comes next in each pattern.

Patterns: Shapes

Name ______________________

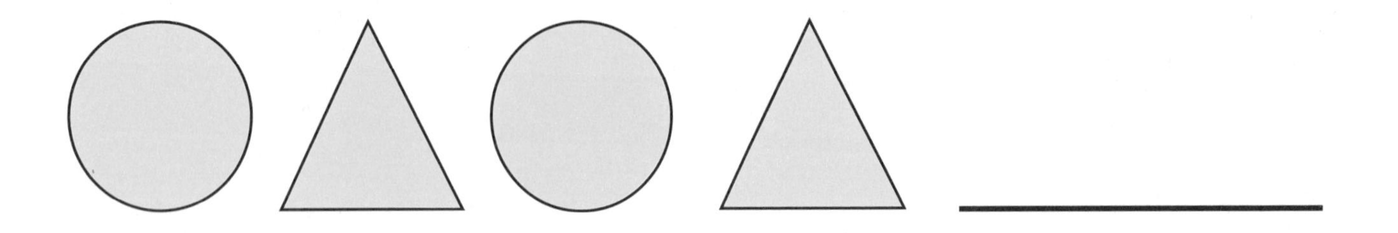

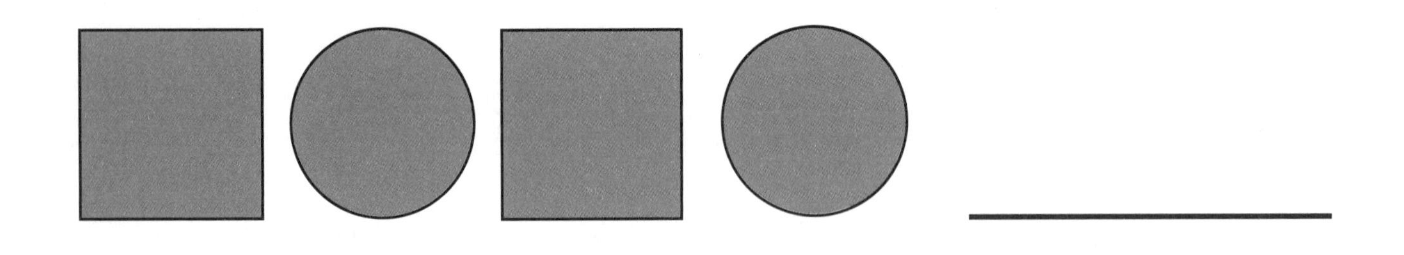

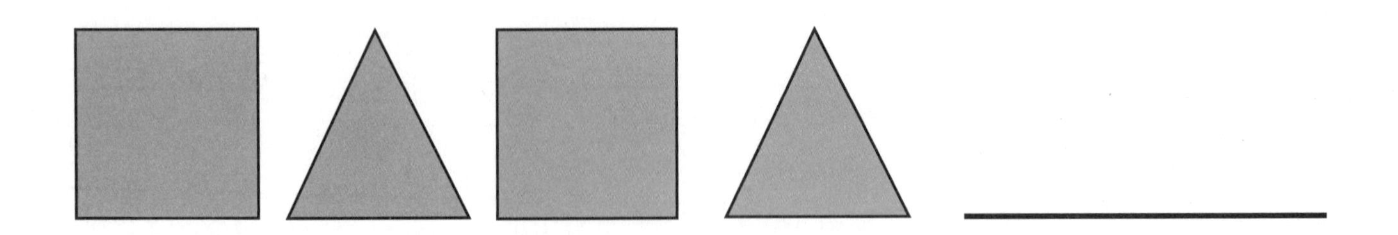

Directions: Draw and color the shape that comes next in each pattern.

Patterns: Shapes

Name

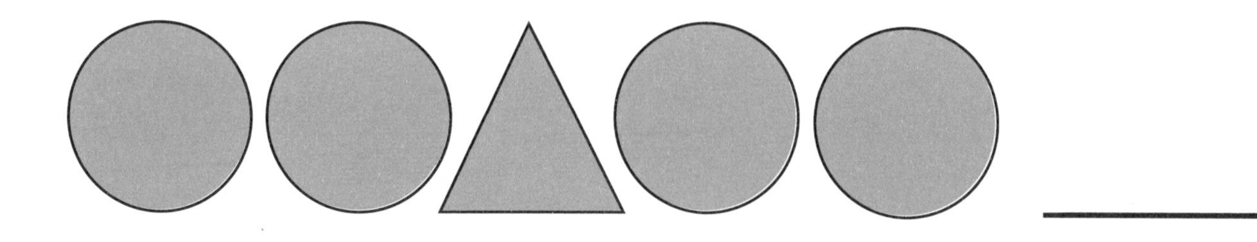

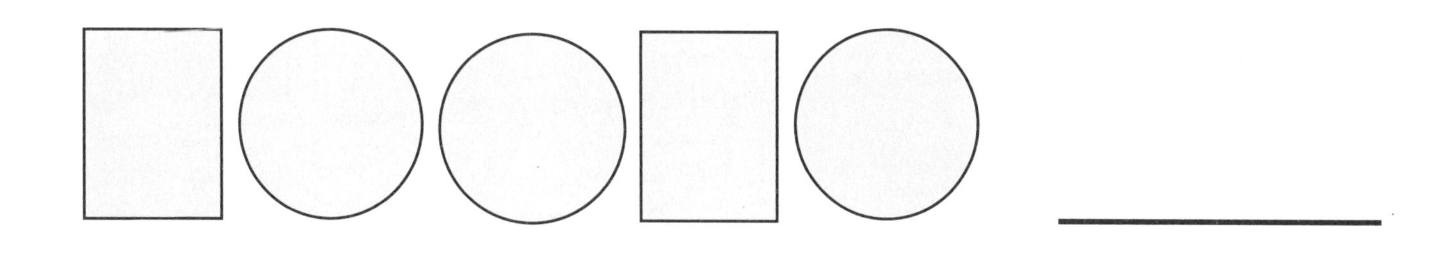

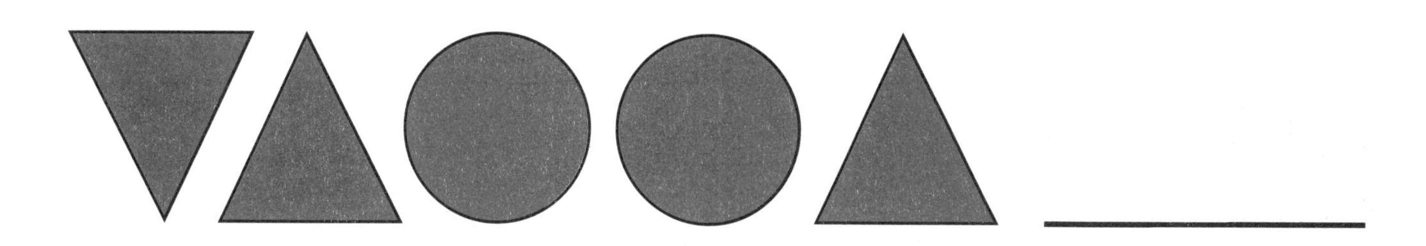

Directions: Draw and color the shape that comes next in each pattern.

Patterns: Colors and Shapes

Name

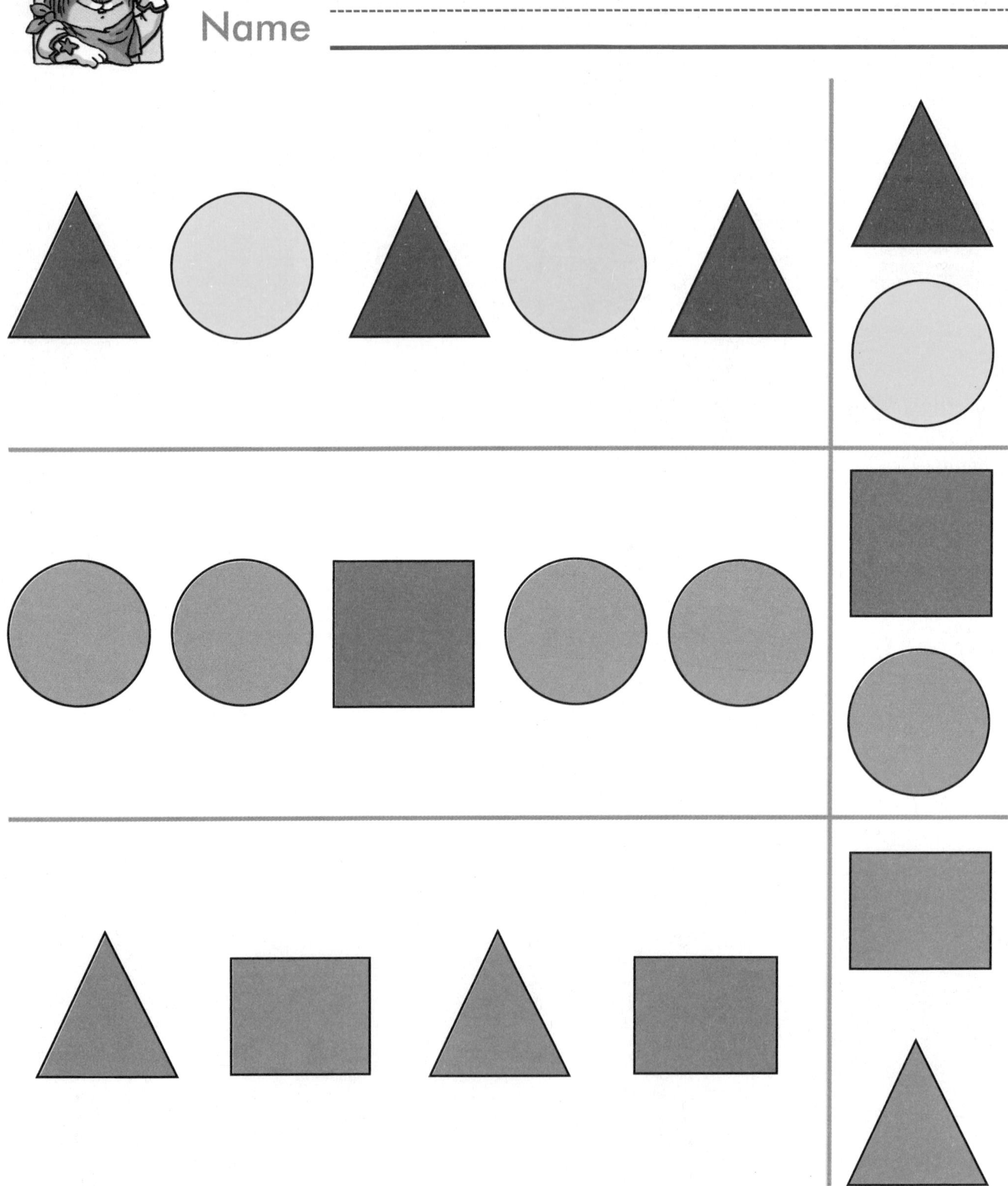

Directions: Circle the shape that comes next in each pattern.

Patterns: Little Critter and Friends

Name

Directions: Have an adult cut out the critters above. Use page 45 to create different patterns with the critters. Keep the cutouts in an envelope so you can use them again.

This page is blank for the
cutting activity on the opposite side
of the page.

Patterns: Little Critter and Friends

Name ______________________

Directions: Have an adult carefully tear out page 43 and cut out the pictures. Then, arrange the pictures in different patterns. Glue some of your patterns to this page.

Zero – 0

Name

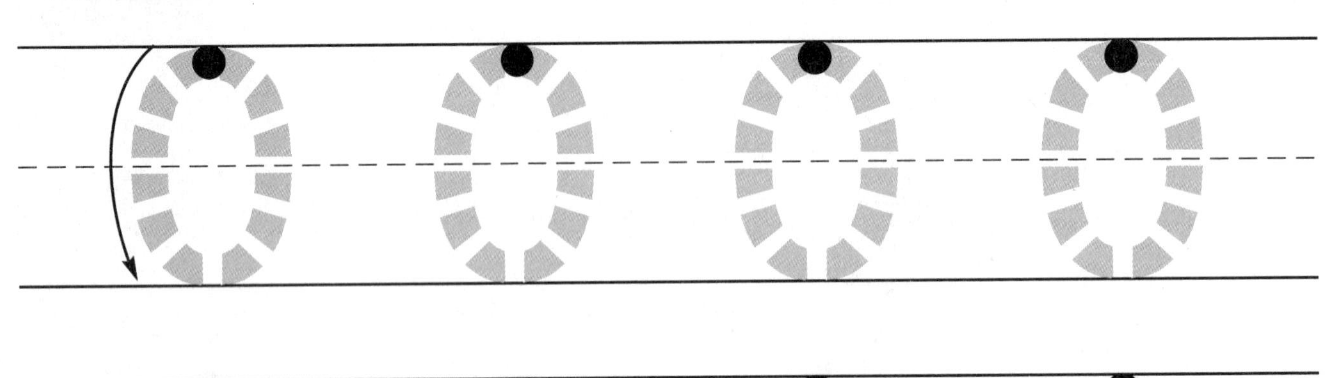

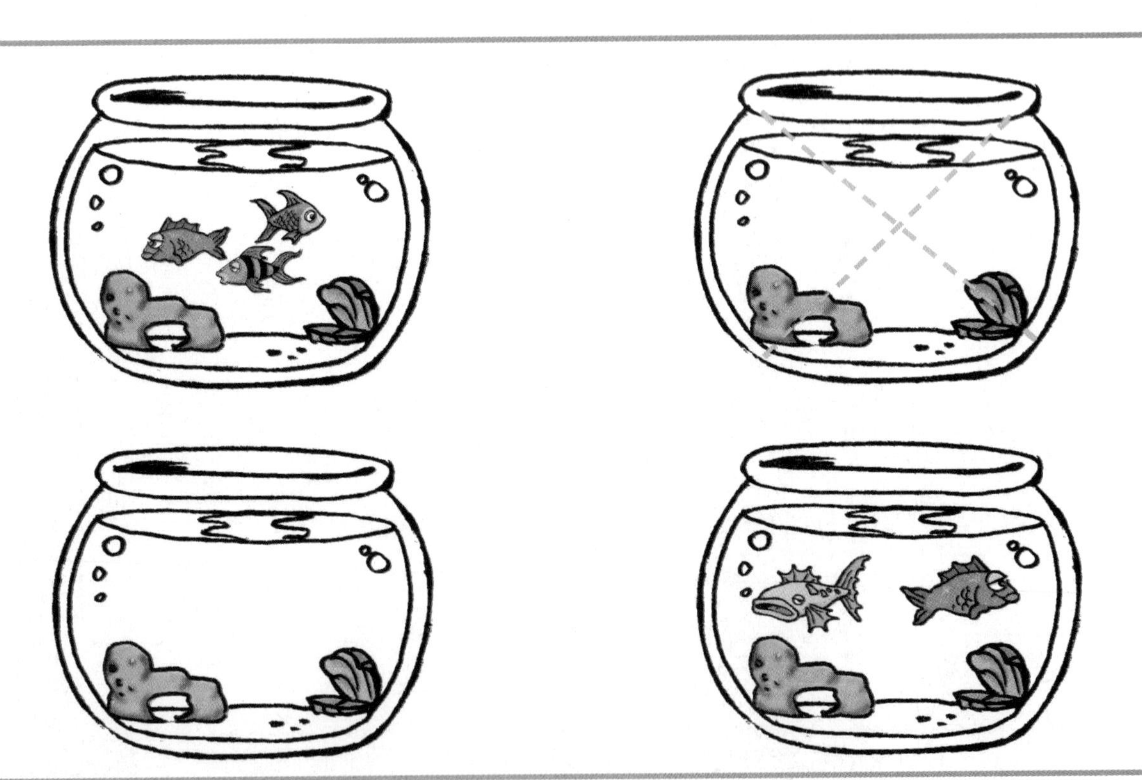

Directions: Trace and write the number 0. Then draw an **X** on each tank with **zero** fish.

One and Two – 1, 2

Name

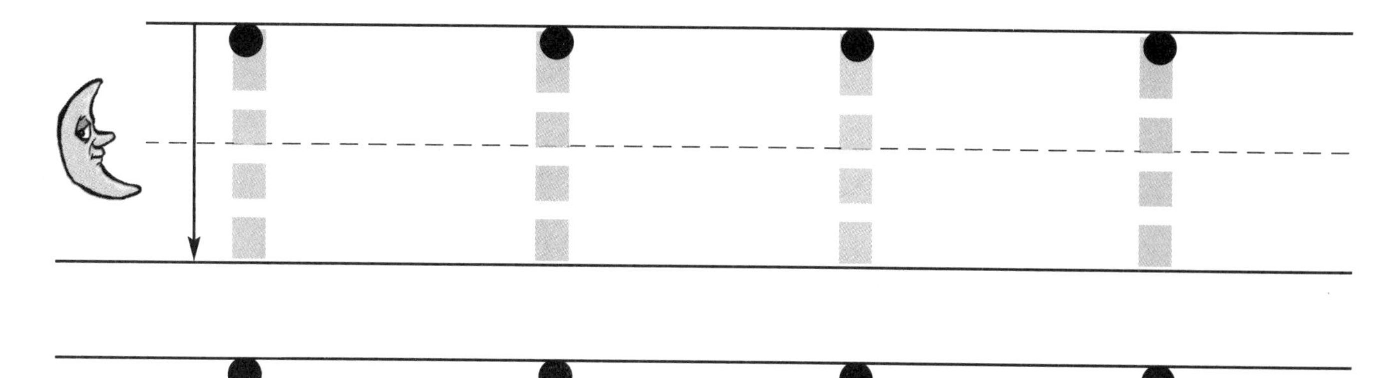

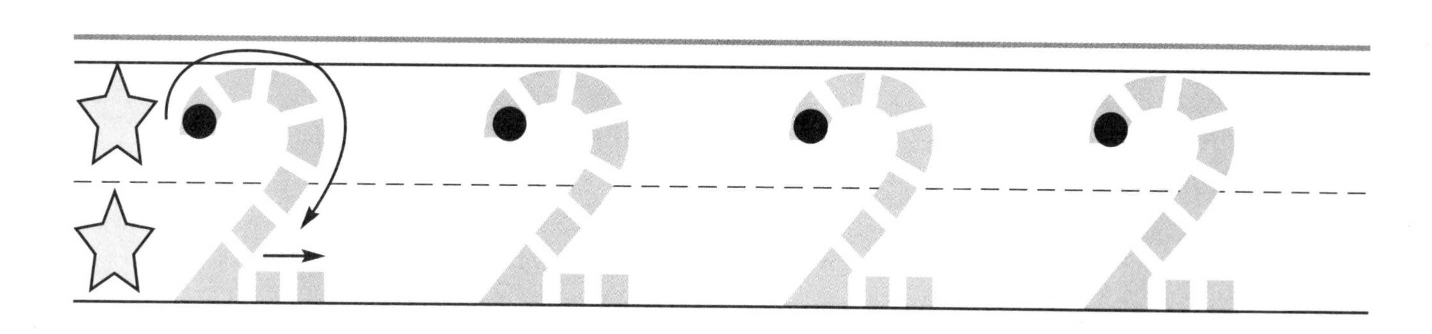

Directions: Trace and write the numbers **1** and **2.**

One and Two

Name

Directions: Count the objects and write the number in each box. Circle the groups of **one.** Color the groups of **two.**

Two – 2

Name ______________________

Directions: Color each space red that has a **2** in it.

Three and Four – 3, 4

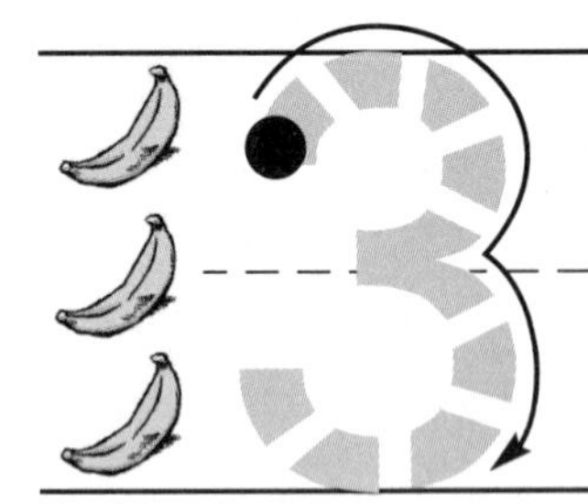

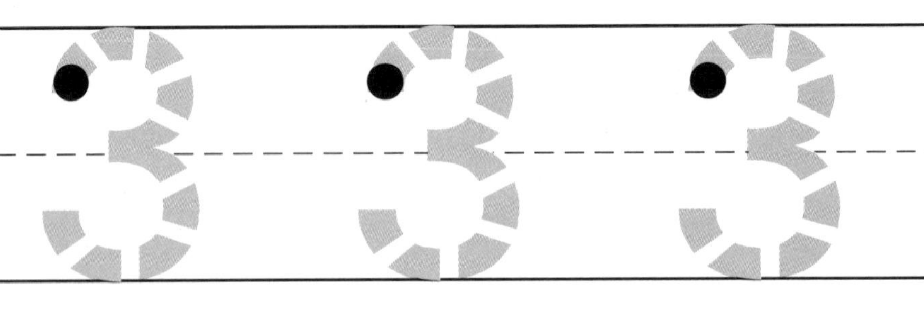

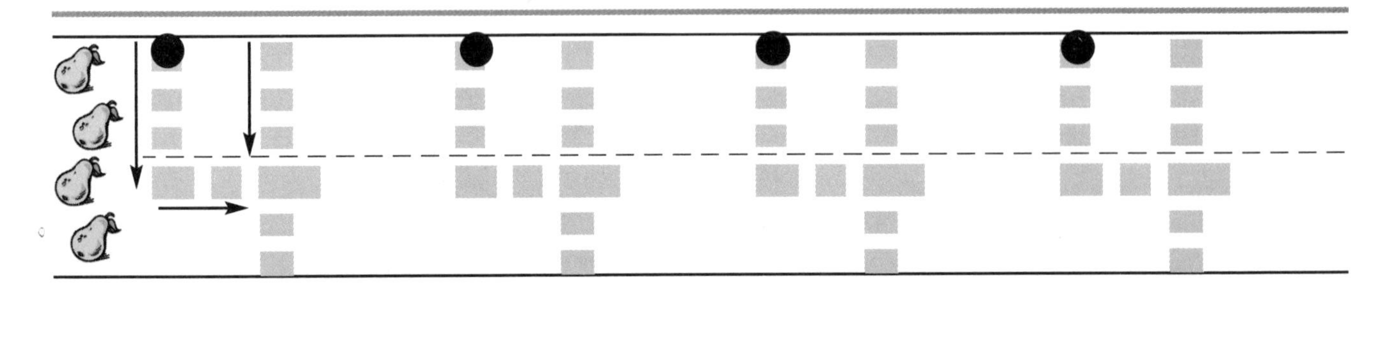

Directions: Trace and write the numbers **3** and **4**.

Three and Four

Name

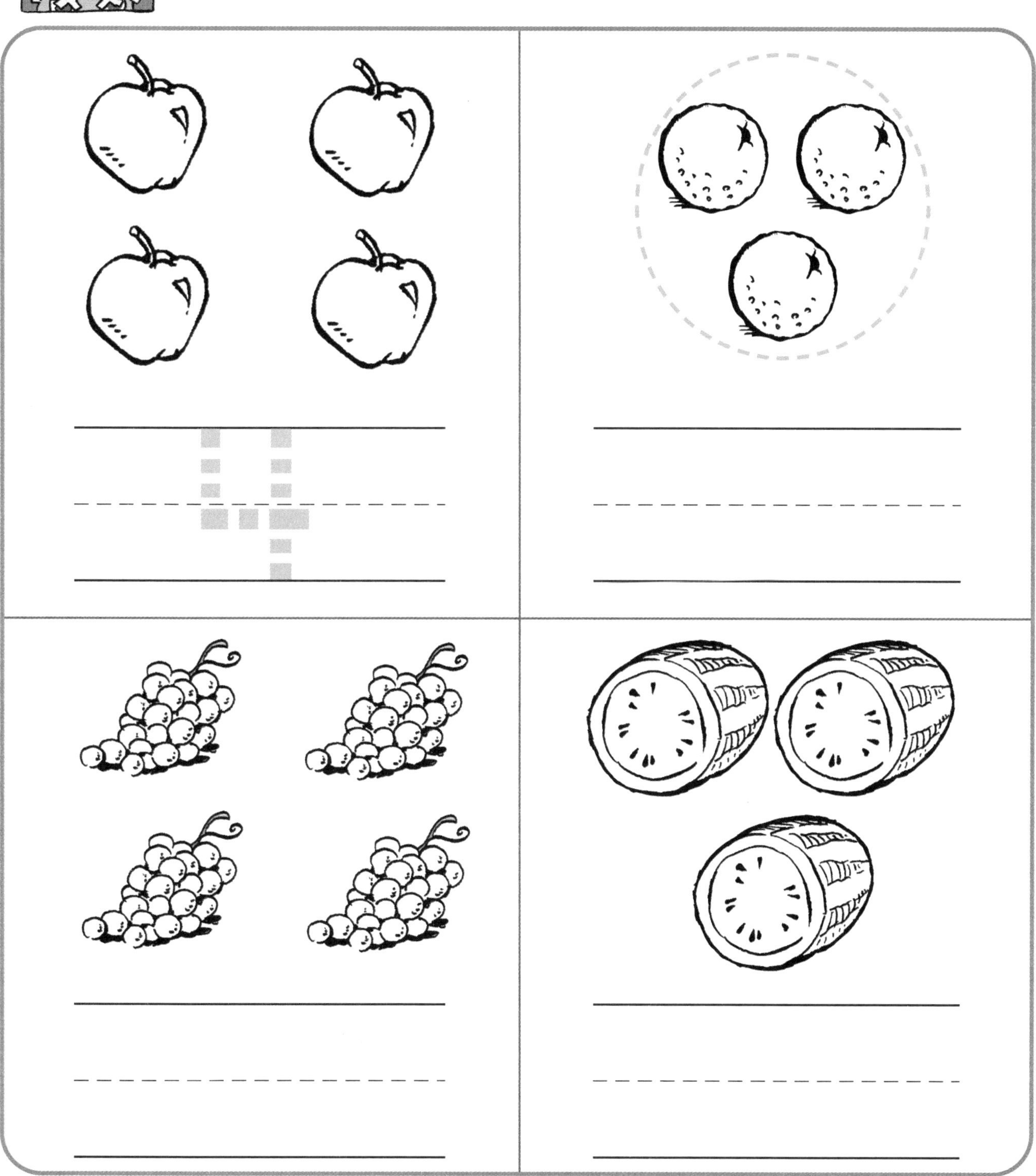

Directions: Count the objects and write the number in each box. Circle the groups of **three.** Color the groups of **four.**

Four

Name ______________________

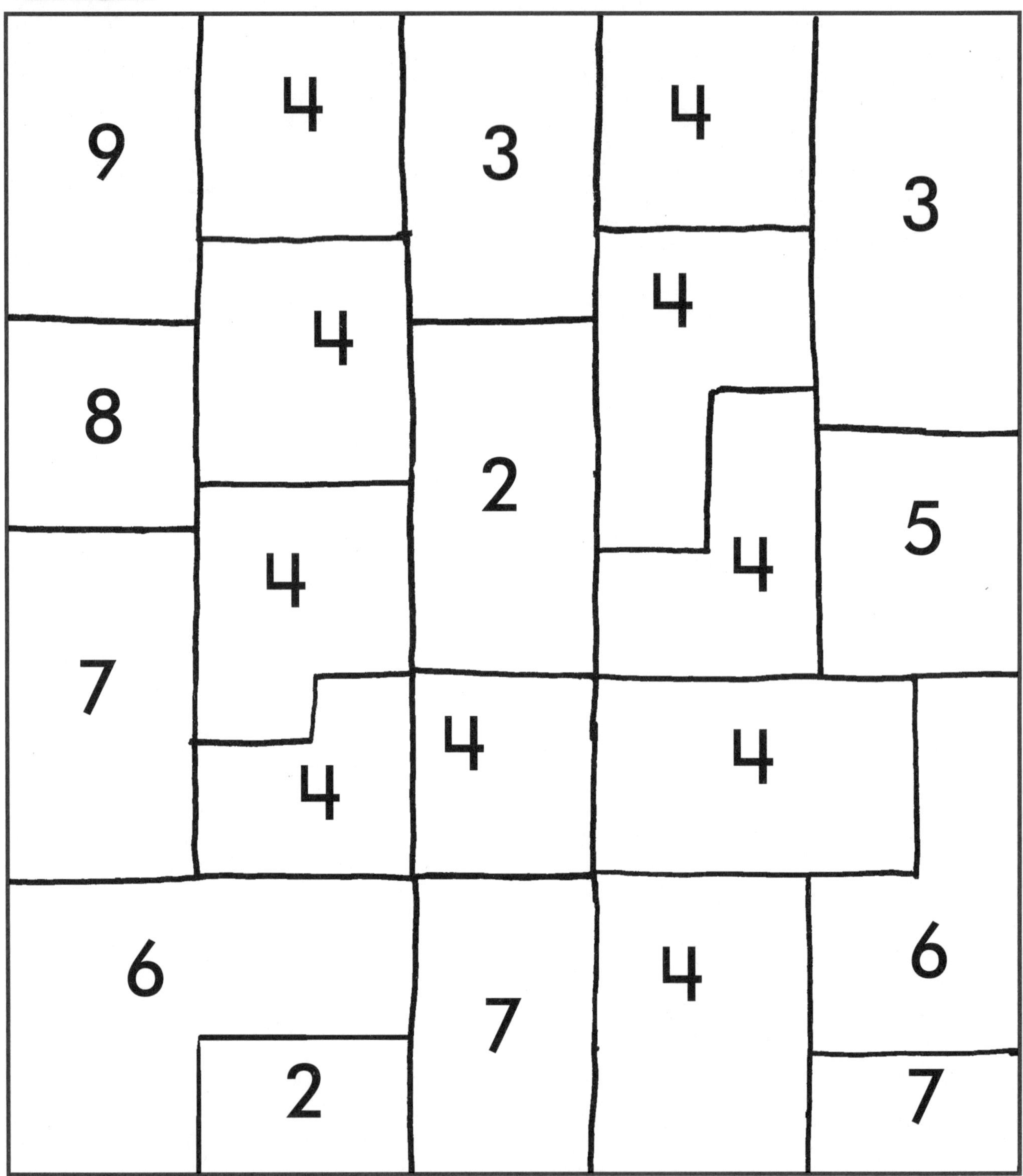

Directions: Color each space blue that has a 4 in it.

Five – 5

Name

5 dogs are colored.
Color five dogs.

Directions: Trace and write the number **5.** Then follow the directions in the box above.

Five

Name ______________________

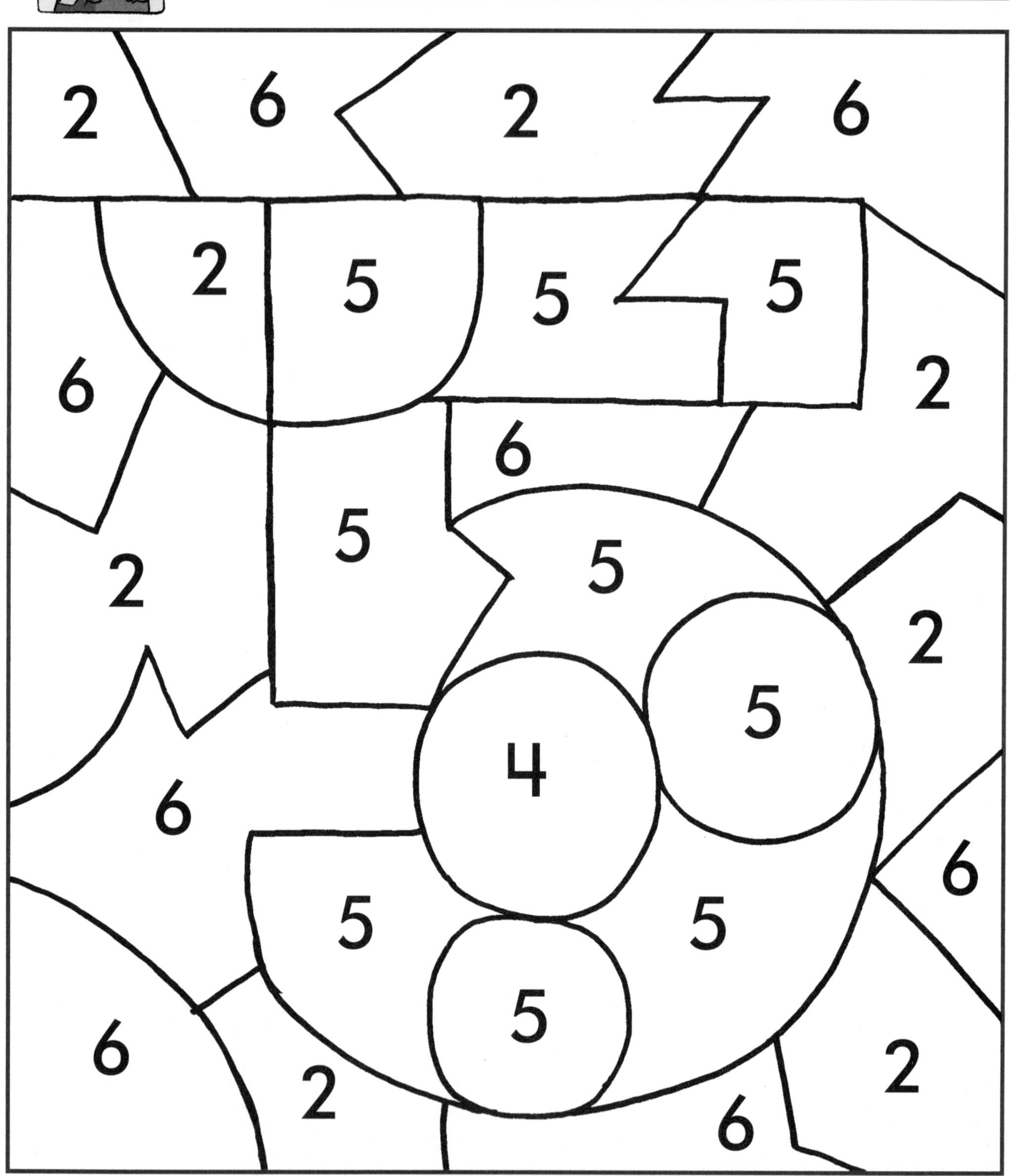

Directions: Color each space green that has a **5** in it.

Numbers 1 to 5: Review

Name ____________________

Directions: Count the balloons in each box. Then write the correct number on the line.

Dot-to-Dot 1 to 5

Name ____________________

Directions: Connect the dots from 1 to 5 to find out where Little Critter and Little Sister are spending the night. Color the picture.

Dot-to-Dot 1 to 5

Name ______________________

Directions: Connect the dots from 1 to 5. Then draw the number of candles you will have on your next birthday cake. Decorate the cake.

Six – 6

Name

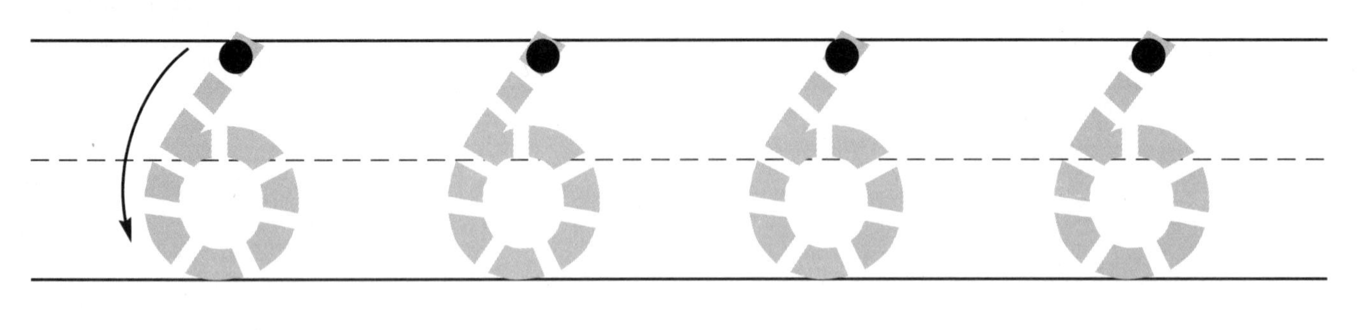

Directions: Trace and write the number **6.** Then draw **six** coins in the piggy bank.

Seven – 7

Name

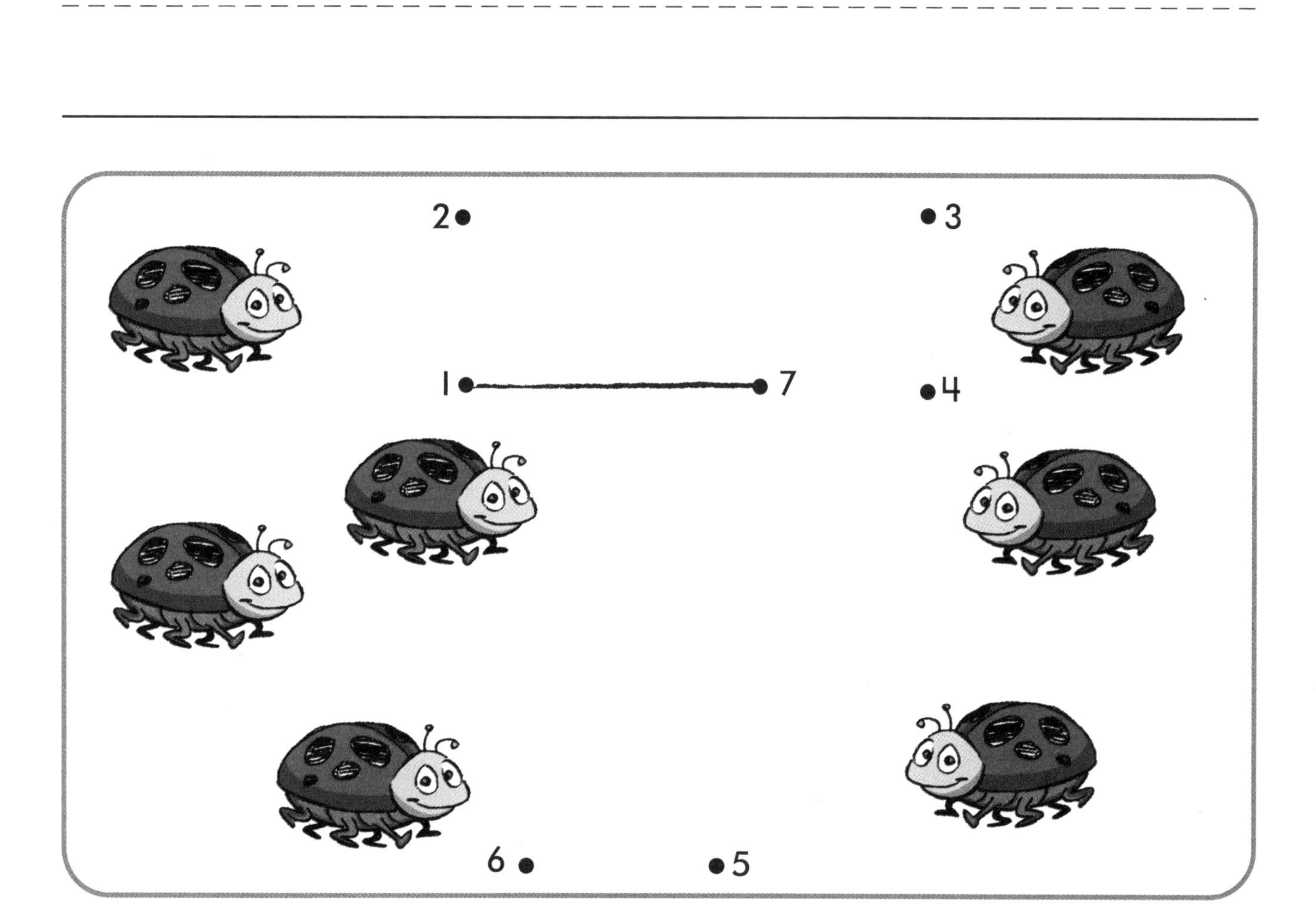

Directions: Trace and write the number **7.** Count the ladybugs. Connect the dots. Then, color the picture.

Dot-to-Dot 1 to 7

Name ______________________________

Directions: Connect the dots from 1 to 7 to find where Blue is sleeping. Color the picture.

Eight – 8

Name

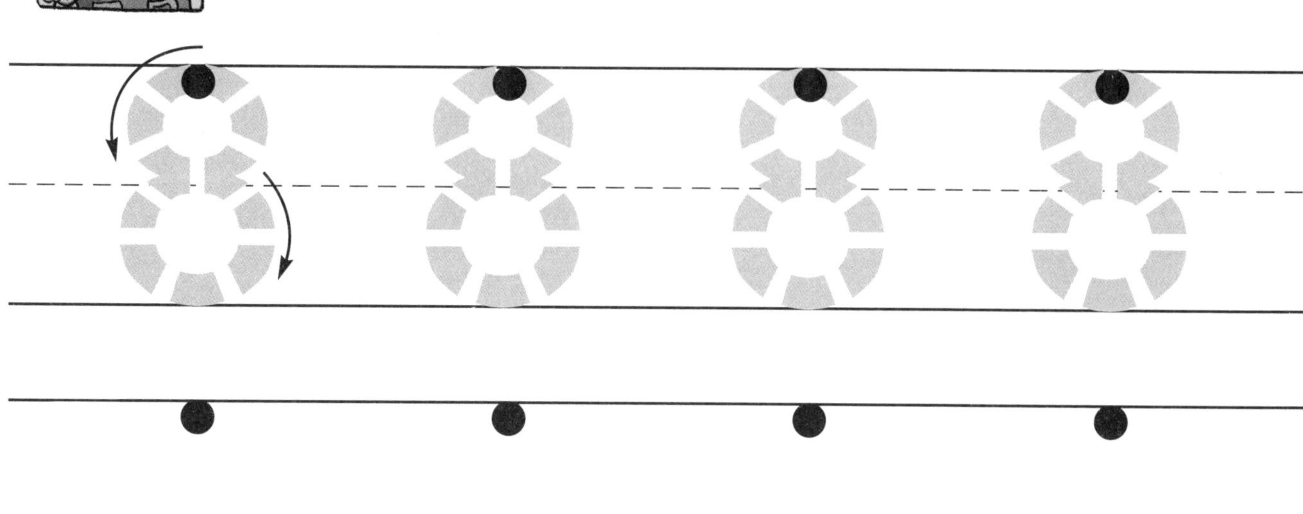

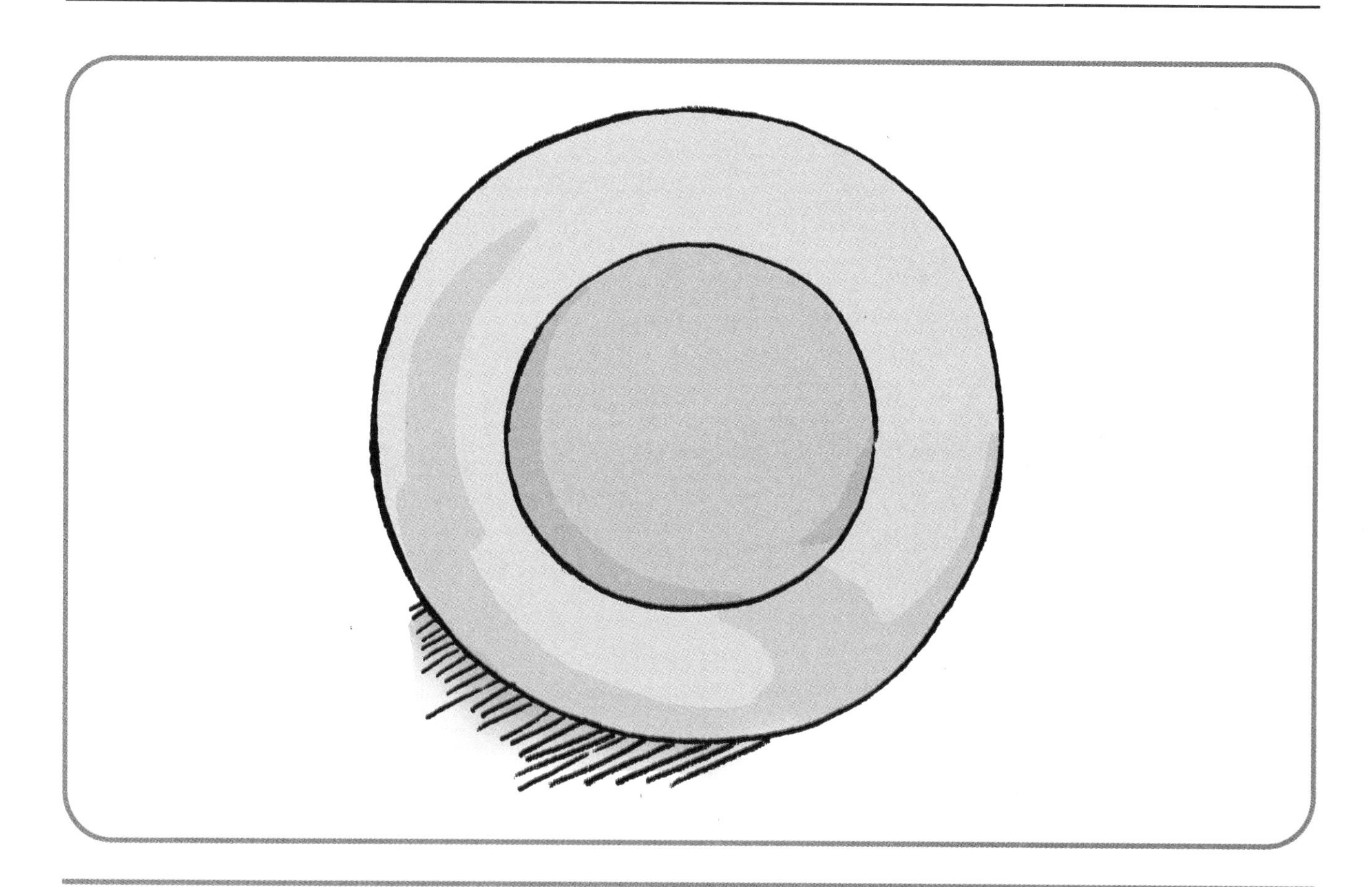

Directions: Trace and write the number **8.** Then draw **eight** peas on the plate.

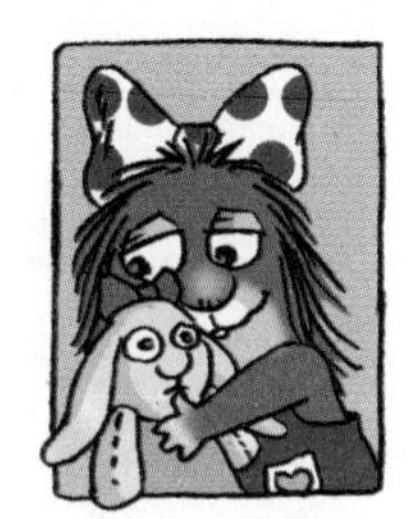

Nine and Ten – 9, 10

Name

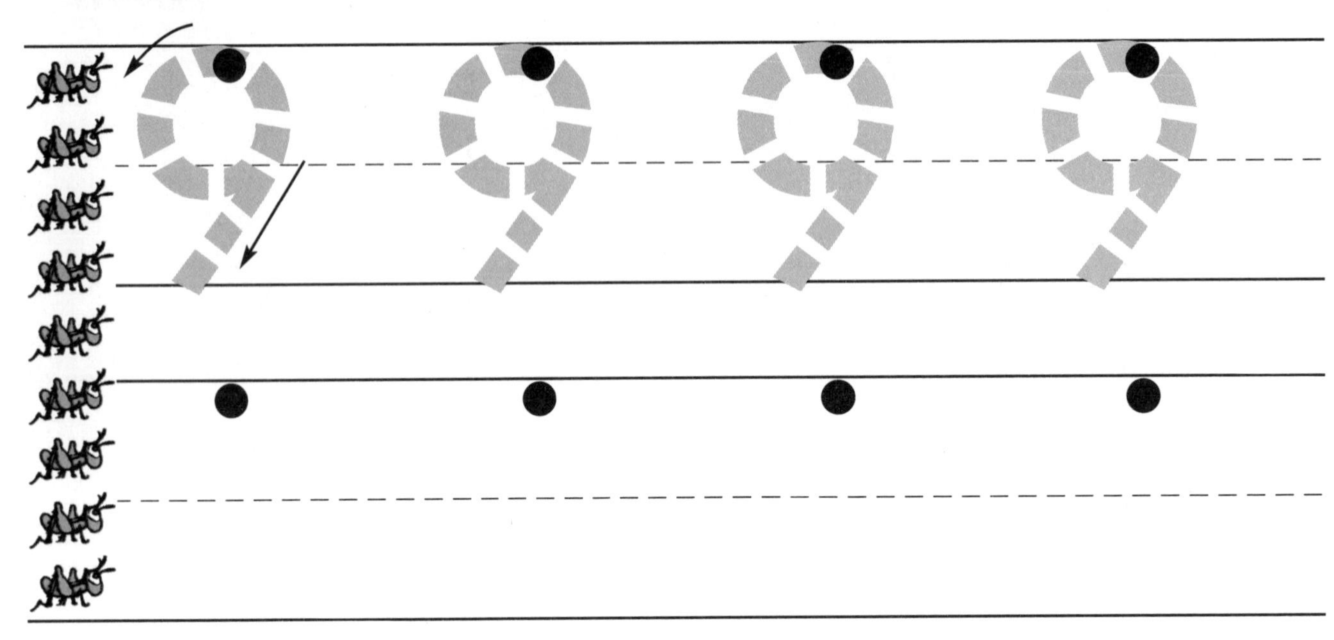

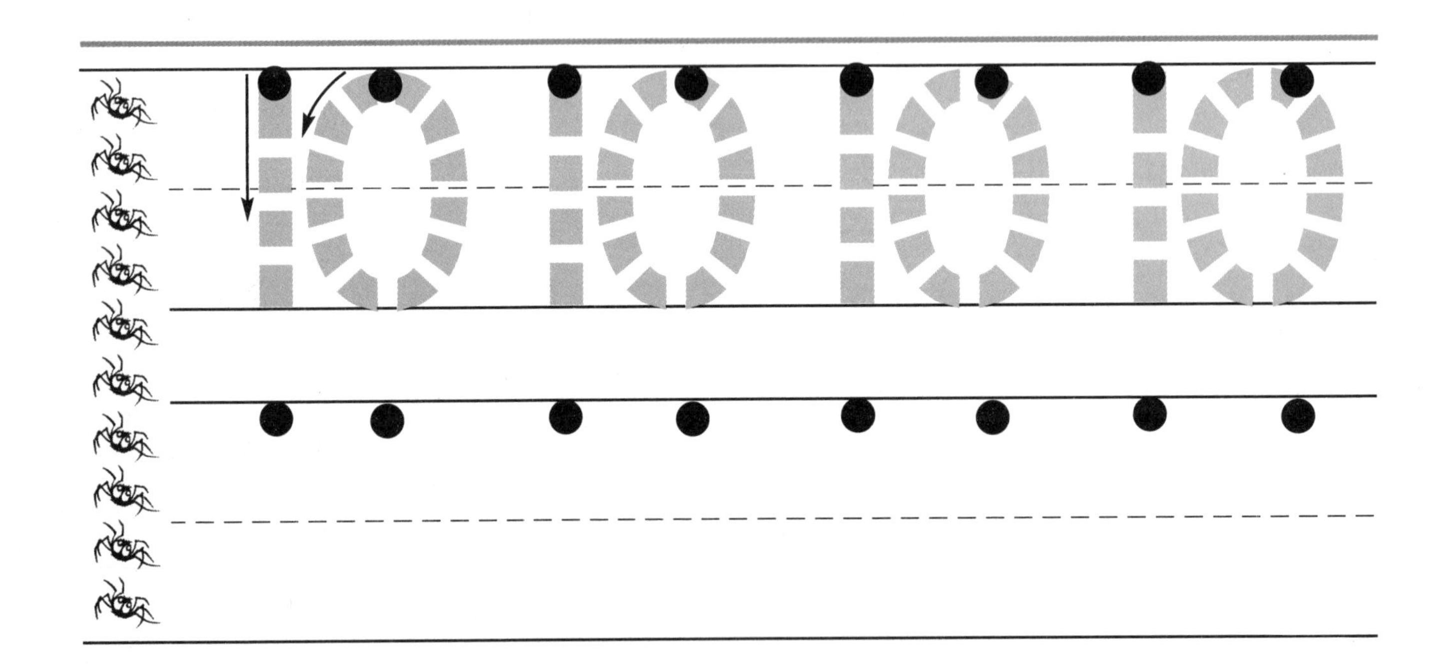

Directions: Trace and write the numbers **9** and **10**.

Nine and Ten

Name

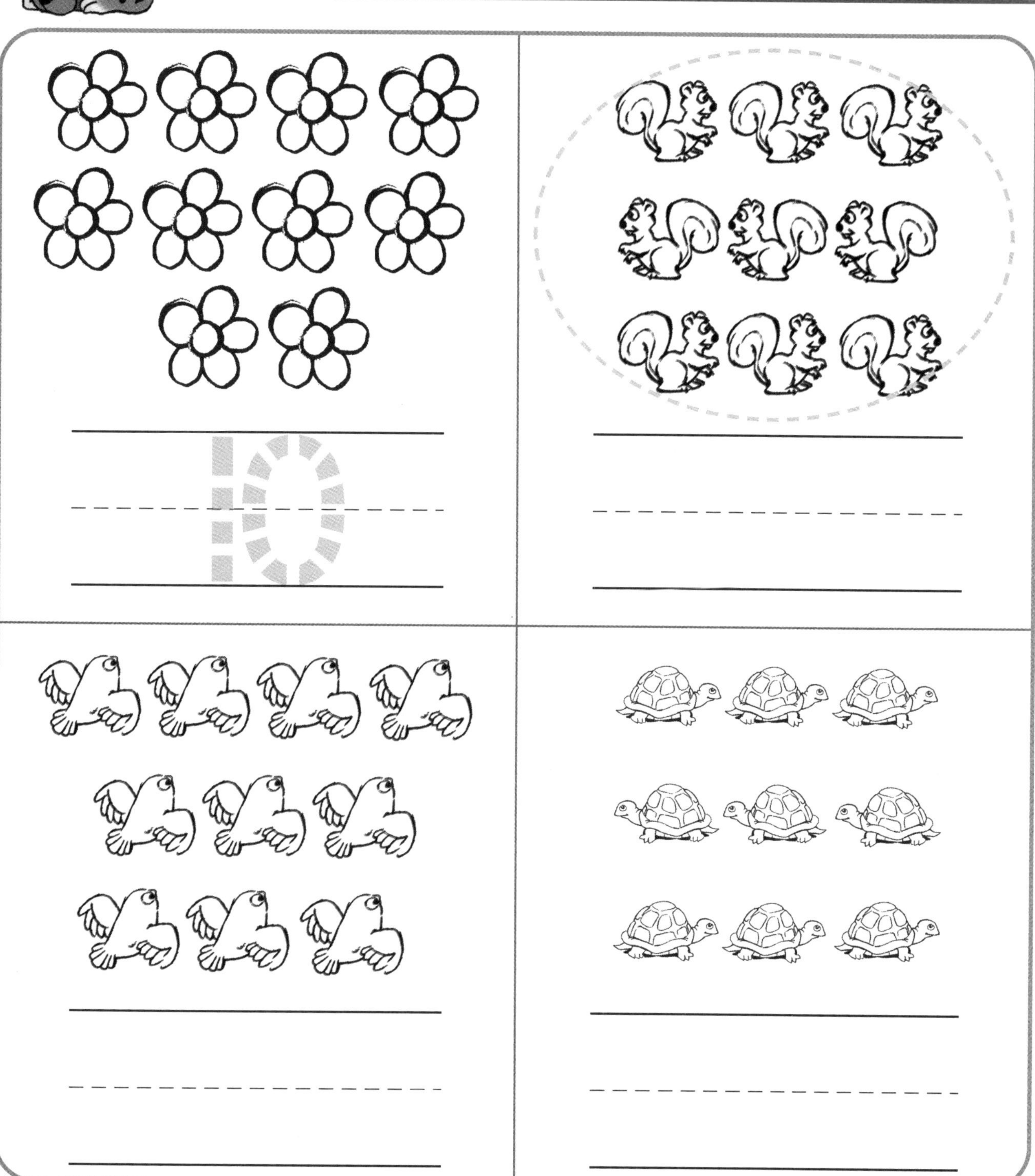

Directions: Count the objects and write the number in each box. Circle the groups of **nine.** Color the groups of **ten.**

Nine

Name

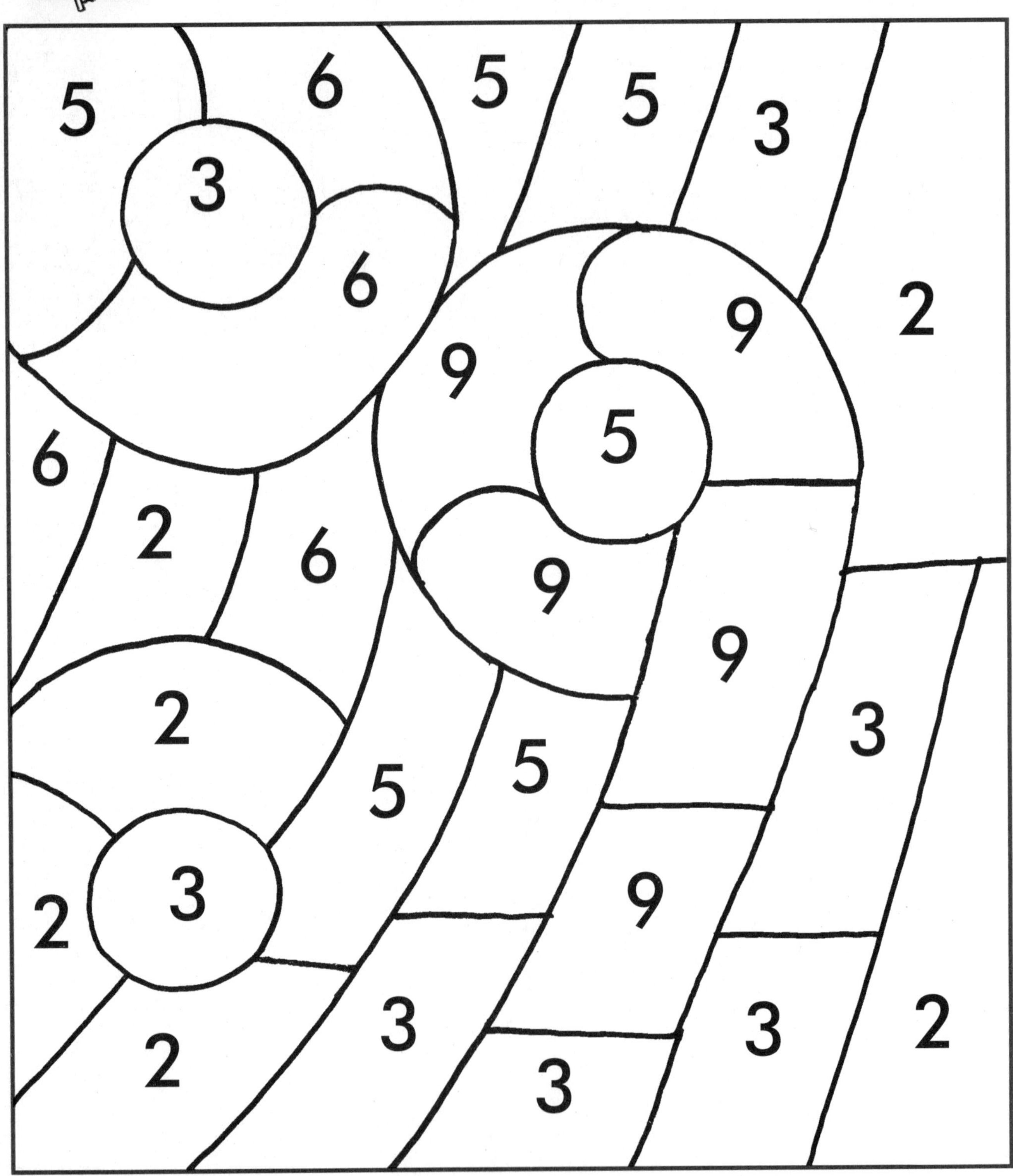

Directions: Color each space orange that has a 9 in it.

Writing Your Telephone Number

Name

Directions: Have an adult write your phone number on the line above. Practice dialing it using the phone in the picture. Then color in the numbers of your phone number on the phone.

Numbers 1 to 10: Review

Name

Directions: Look at Little Sister's hopscotch board. Help her fill in the missing numbers.

Dot-to-Dot 1 to 10

Name

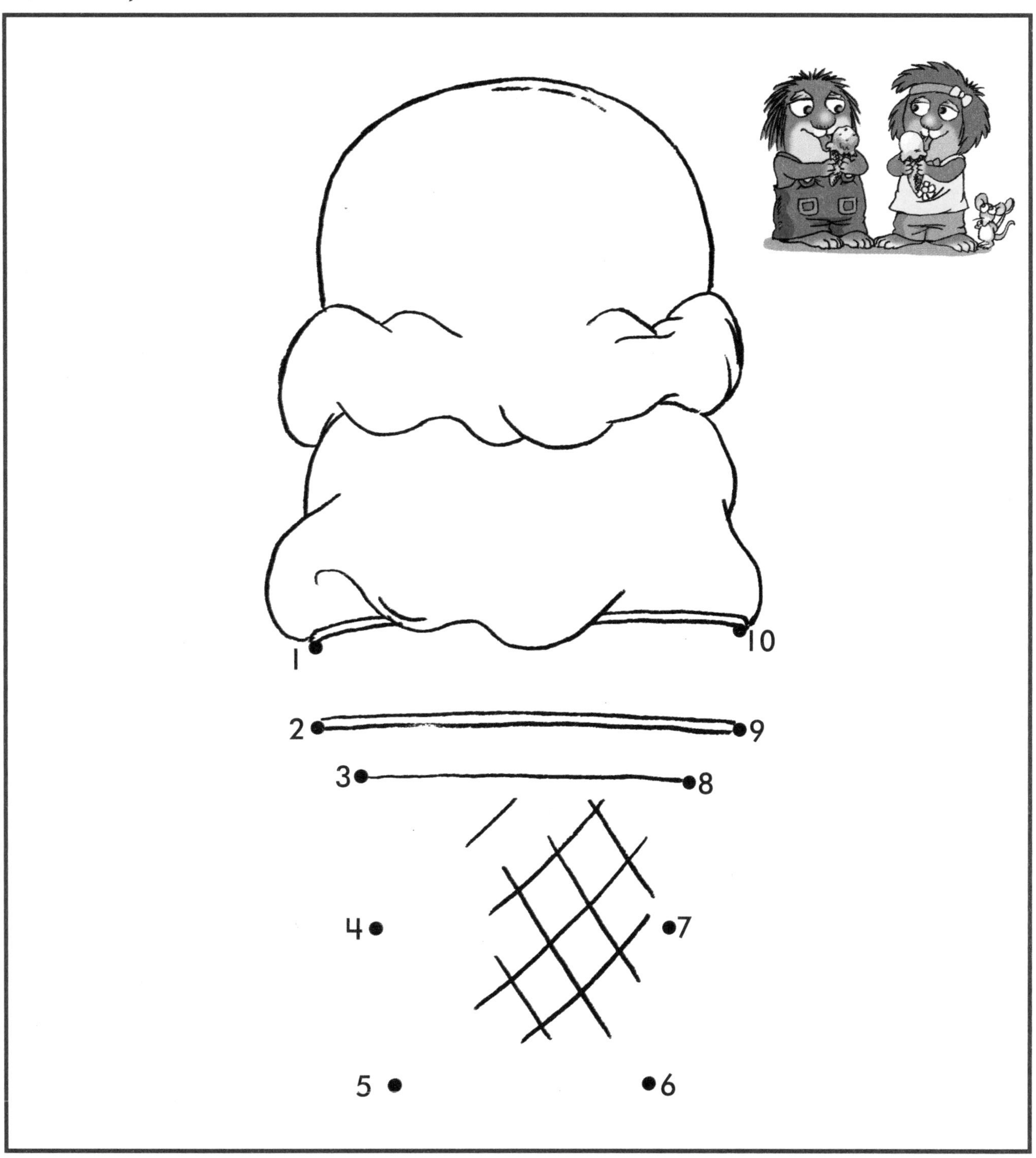

Directions: Connect the dots from 1 to 10 to find Little Critter and Gabby's favorite treat. Color the picture.

Numbers 1 to 10: Review

Name

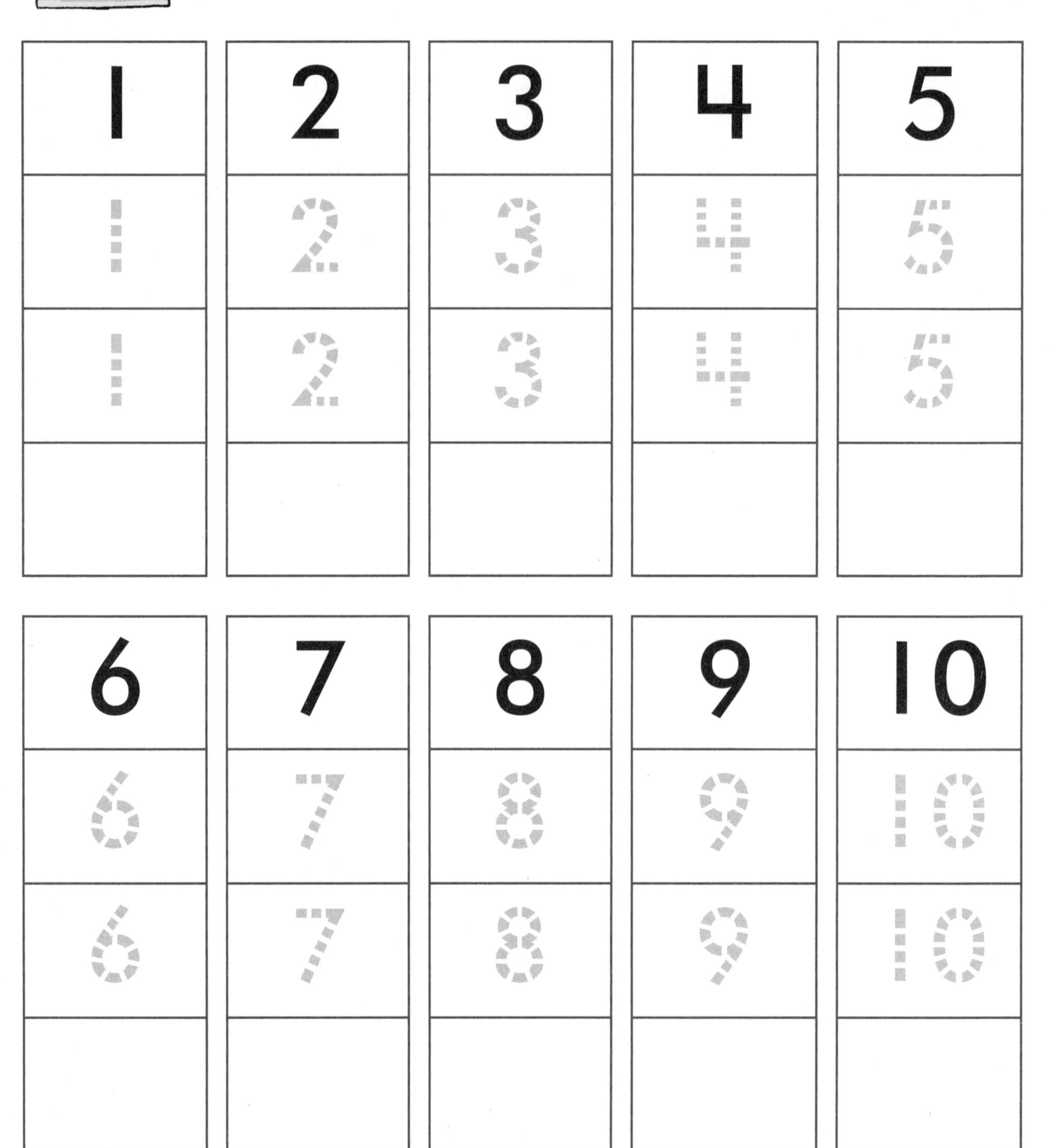

Directions: Read the numbers in the first row. Then trace the numbers in the next two rows. In the last row, write the numbers on your own.

Number Matching

Name

1	2
9	1
3	3
2	5
4	9
5	4
7	8
6	7
8	6

Directions: Draw a line to the matching numbers.

Number Practice 1 to 20

Name Moira

1	2	
3	4	5
6	7	8
9	10	11
12	13	14
15	16	17
18	19	20

Directions: Say the name of each number as you trace it. How high can you count?

Dot-to-Dot 1 to 20

Name ______________________

Directions: Connect the dots from 1 to 20 to find what Little Critter builds at the beach. Color the picture.

What Comes Next?

Name ________________

Directions: What comes next? Write the number on the line.

What Comes Next?

Name

Directions: What comes next? Write the number on the line.

Ordinal Numbers: First

Name ______________________________

Directions: Circle the **first** picture in each row.

Ordinal Numbers: Second

Name ____________________

Directions: Circle the **second** picture in each row.

Ordinal Numbers: Third

Name ______________________

Directions: Circle the **third** picture in each row.

Ordinal Numbers: Fourth

Name ______________________

Directions: Circle the **fourth** picture in each row.

Ordinal Numbers: Fifth

Name

    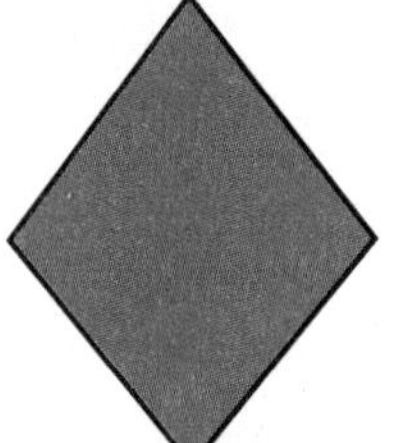 

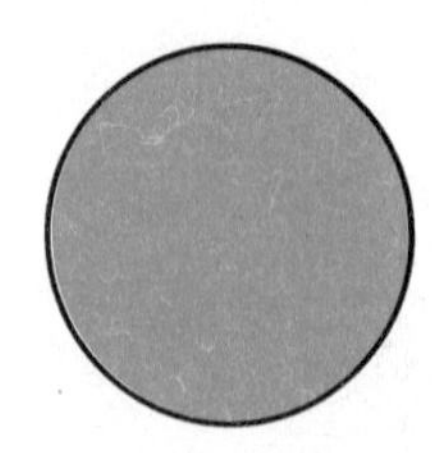 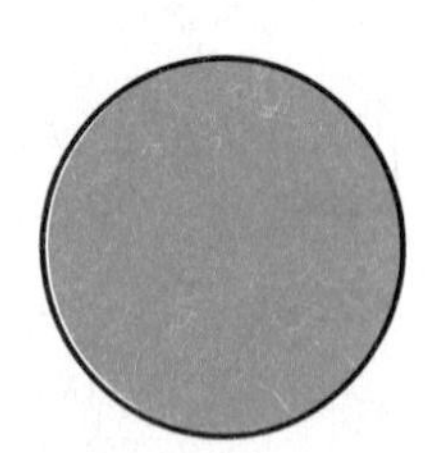 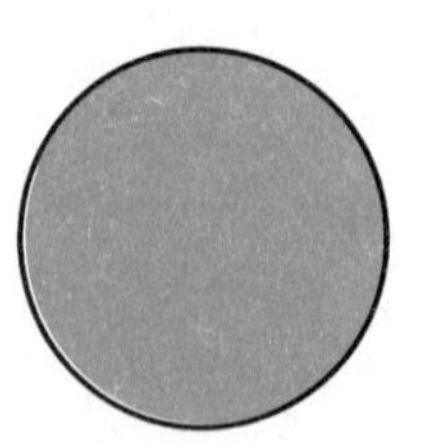 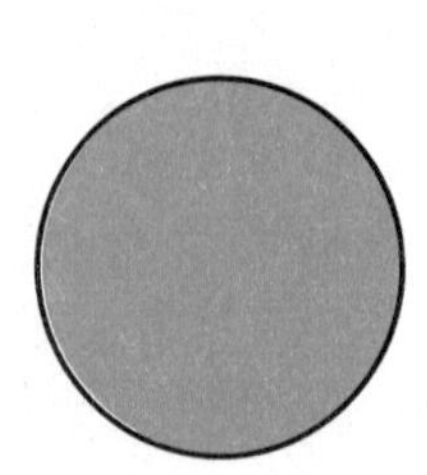 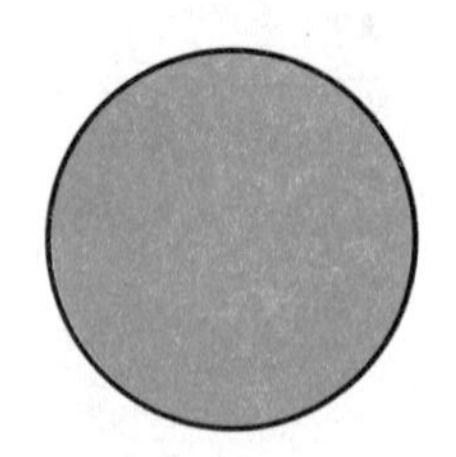

Directions: Circle the **fifth** picture in each row.

Ordinal Numbers: Review

Name

Color the **first** leaf red. Circle the **third** leaf.

Color the **fourth** balloon purple. Draw a line under the **second** balloon.

Follow the directions in each row above.

Fewer

Name

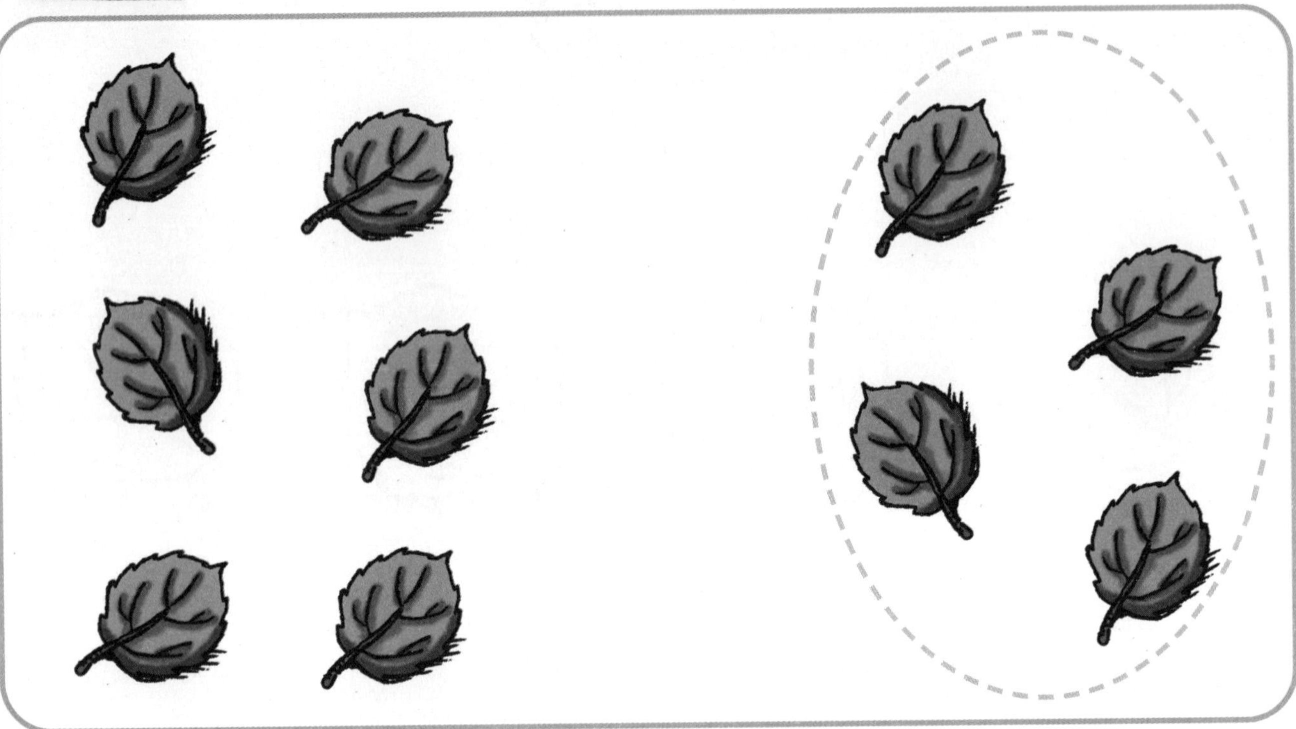

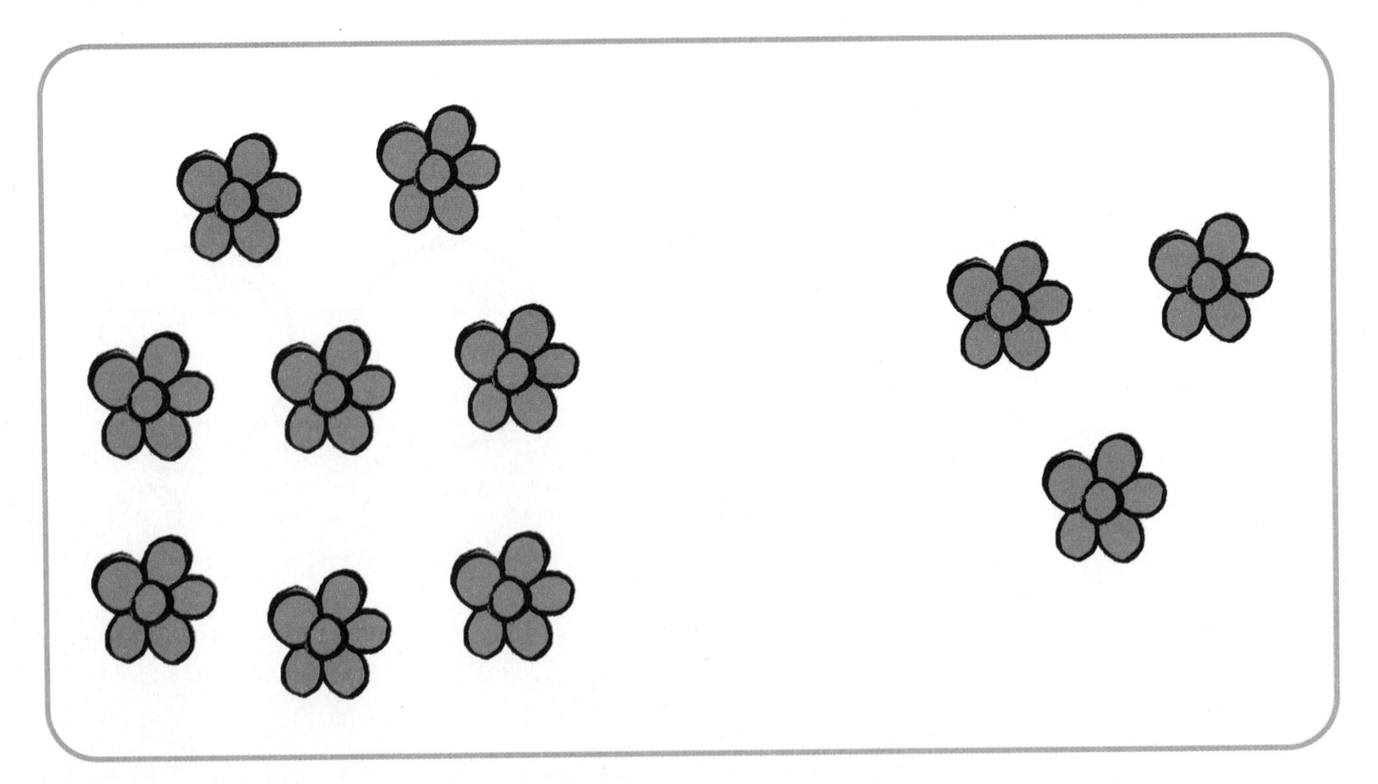

Directions: Circle the group in each box that has **fewer.**

Fewer

Name

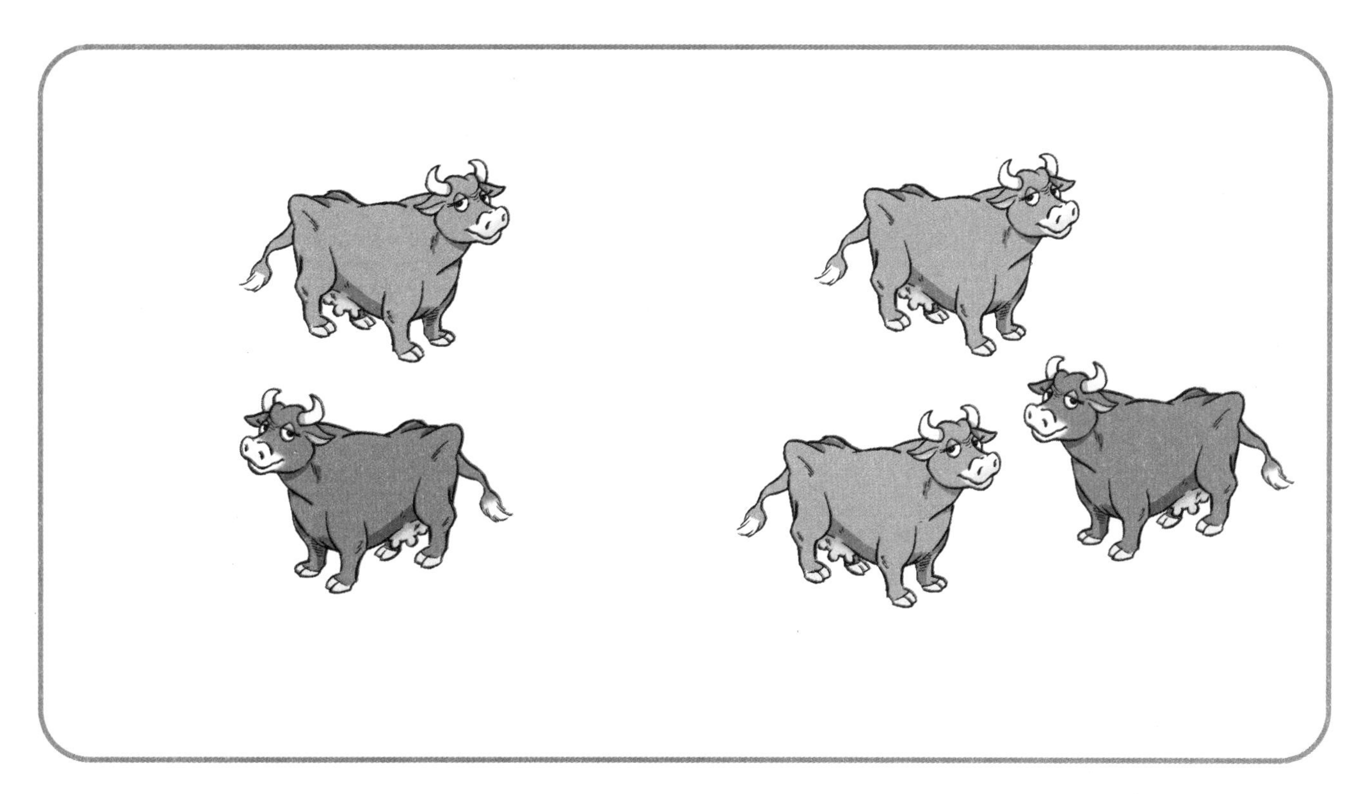

Directions: Circle the group in each box that has **fewer.**

Fewer

Name

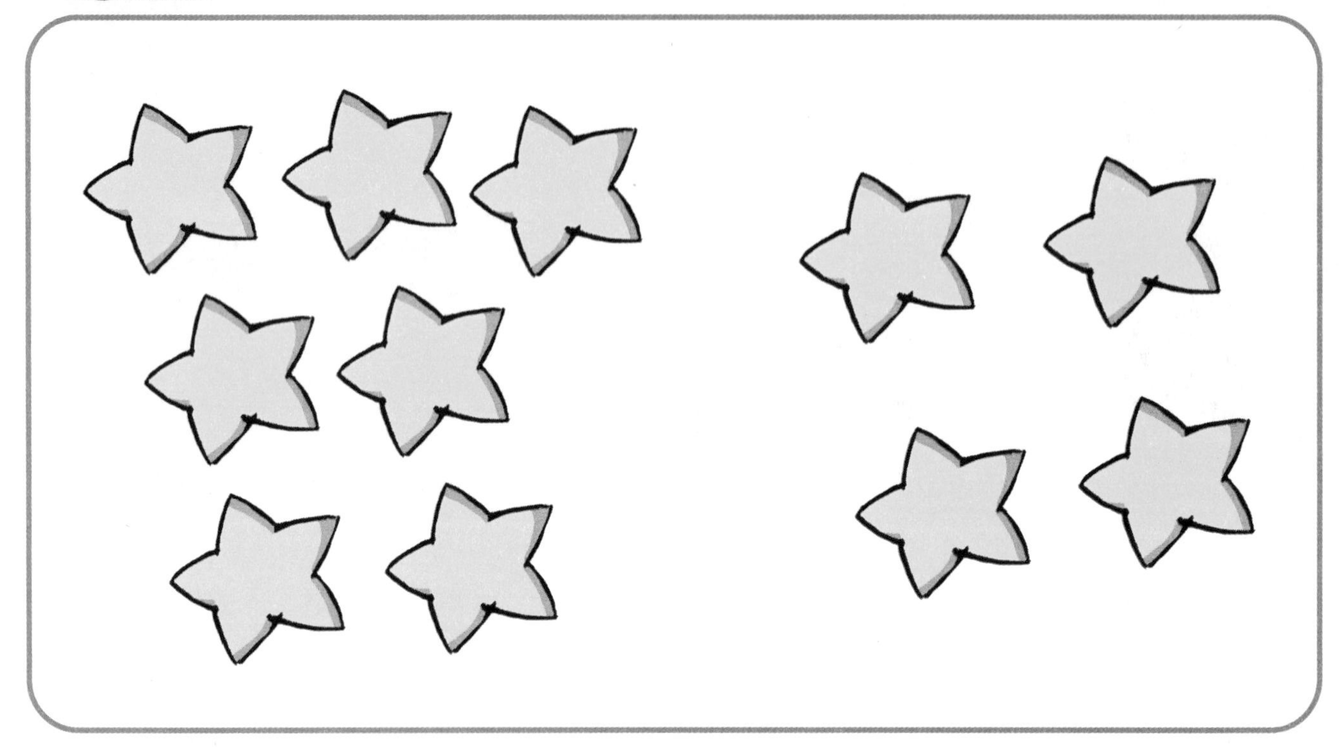

Directions: Circle the group in each box that has **fewer.**

More

Name

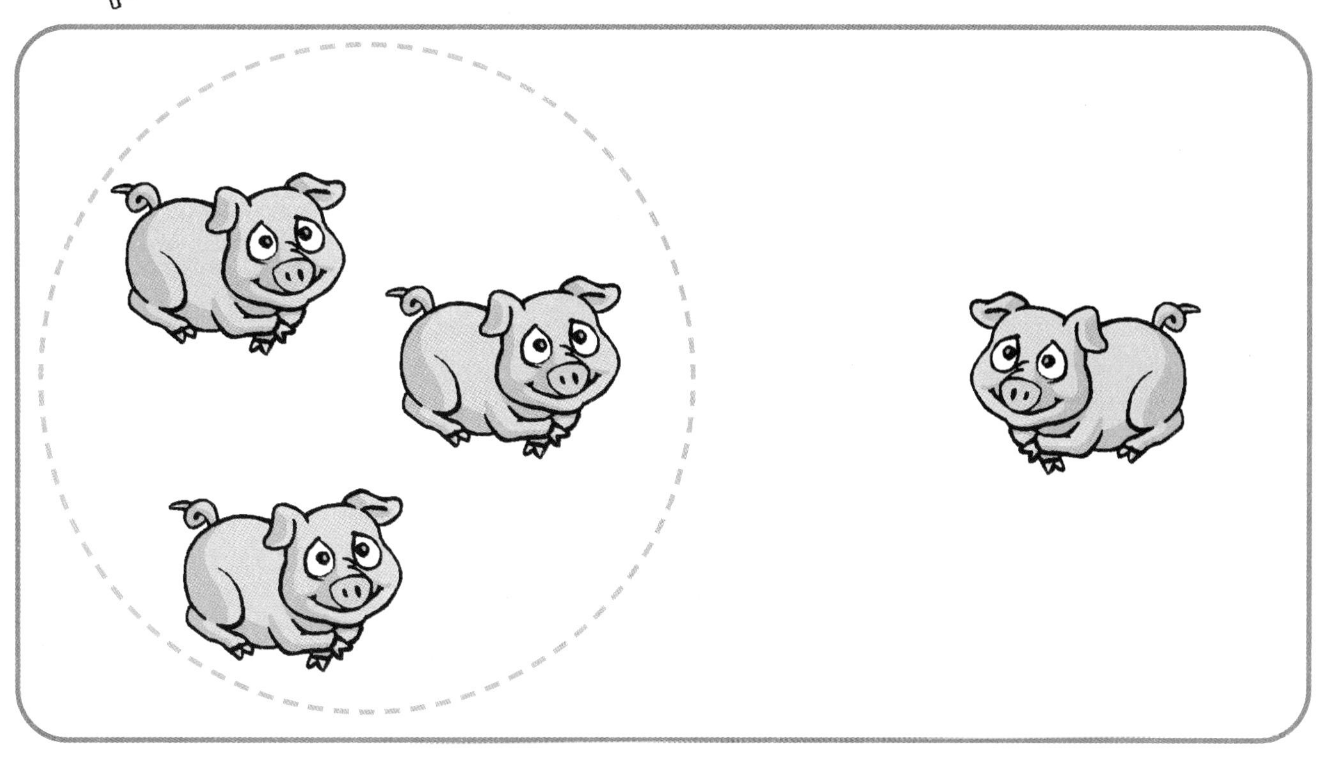

Directions: Circle the group in each box that has **more.**

More

Name

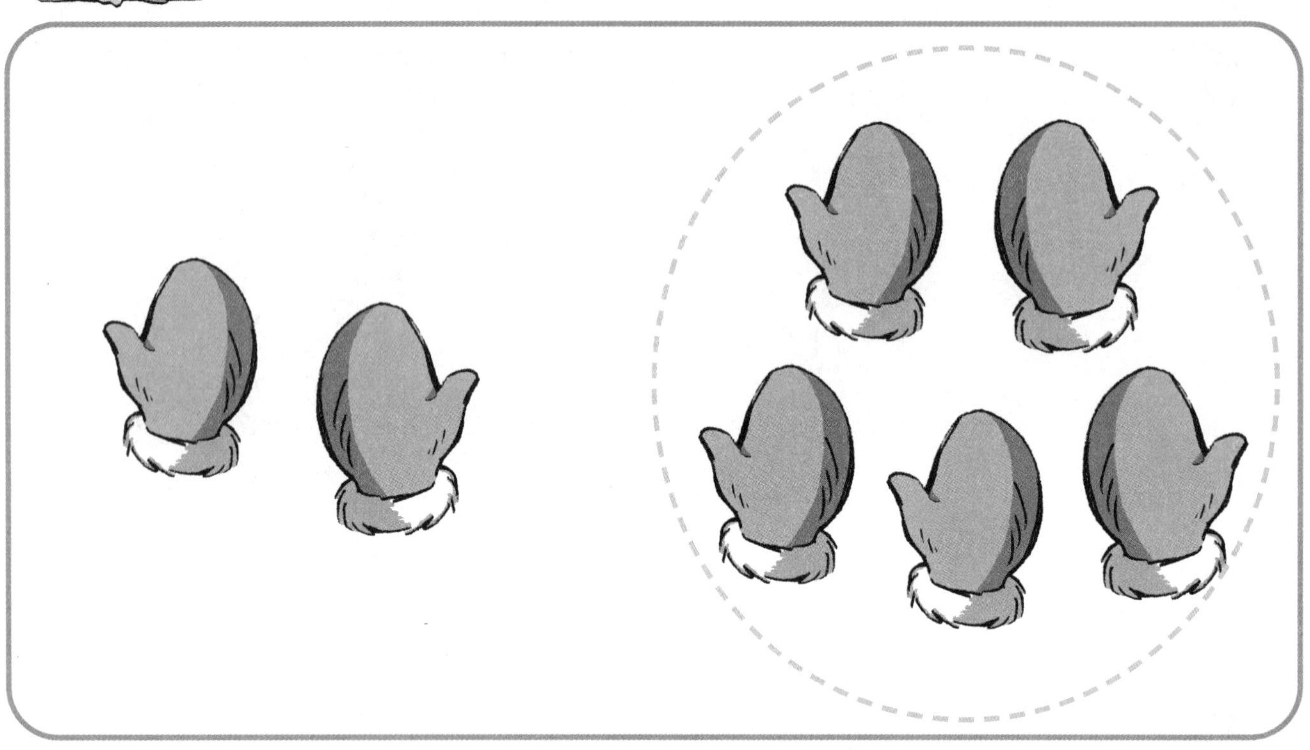

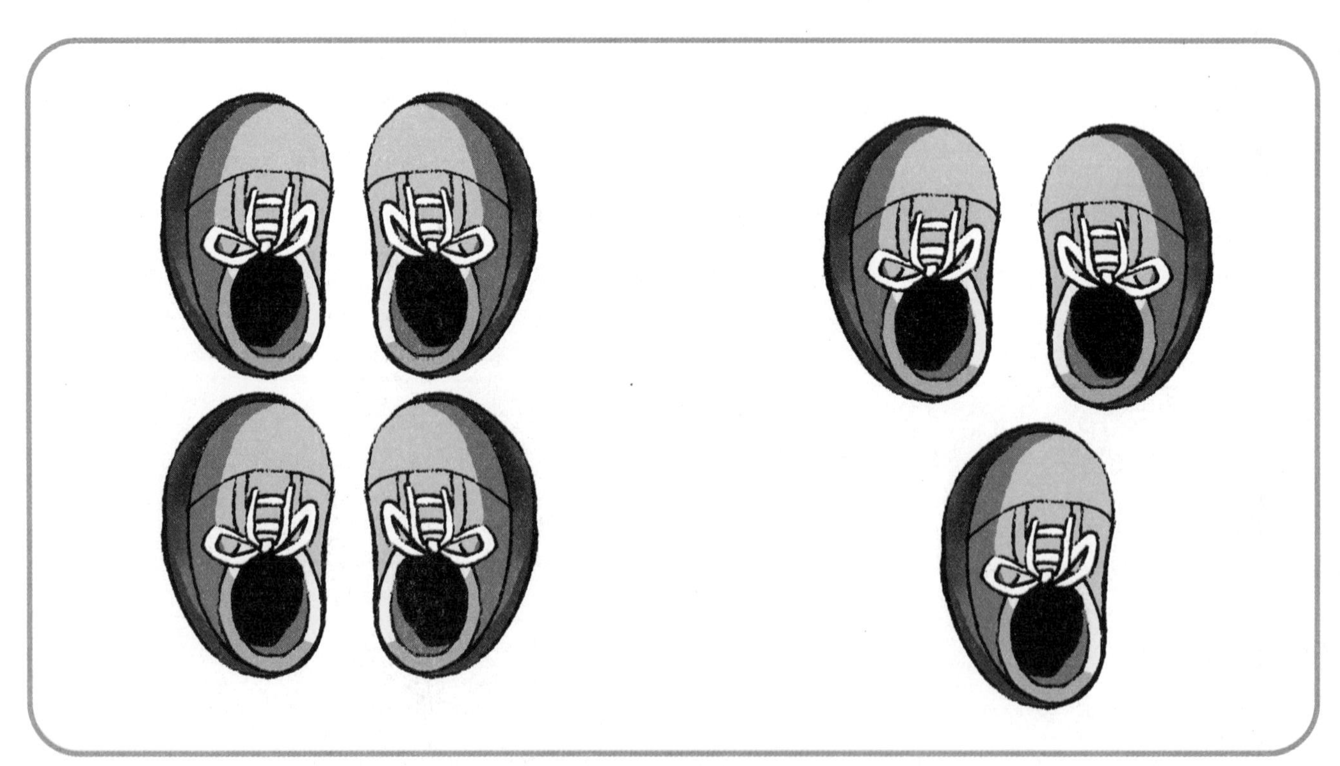

Directions: Circle the group in each box that has **more.**

More

Name

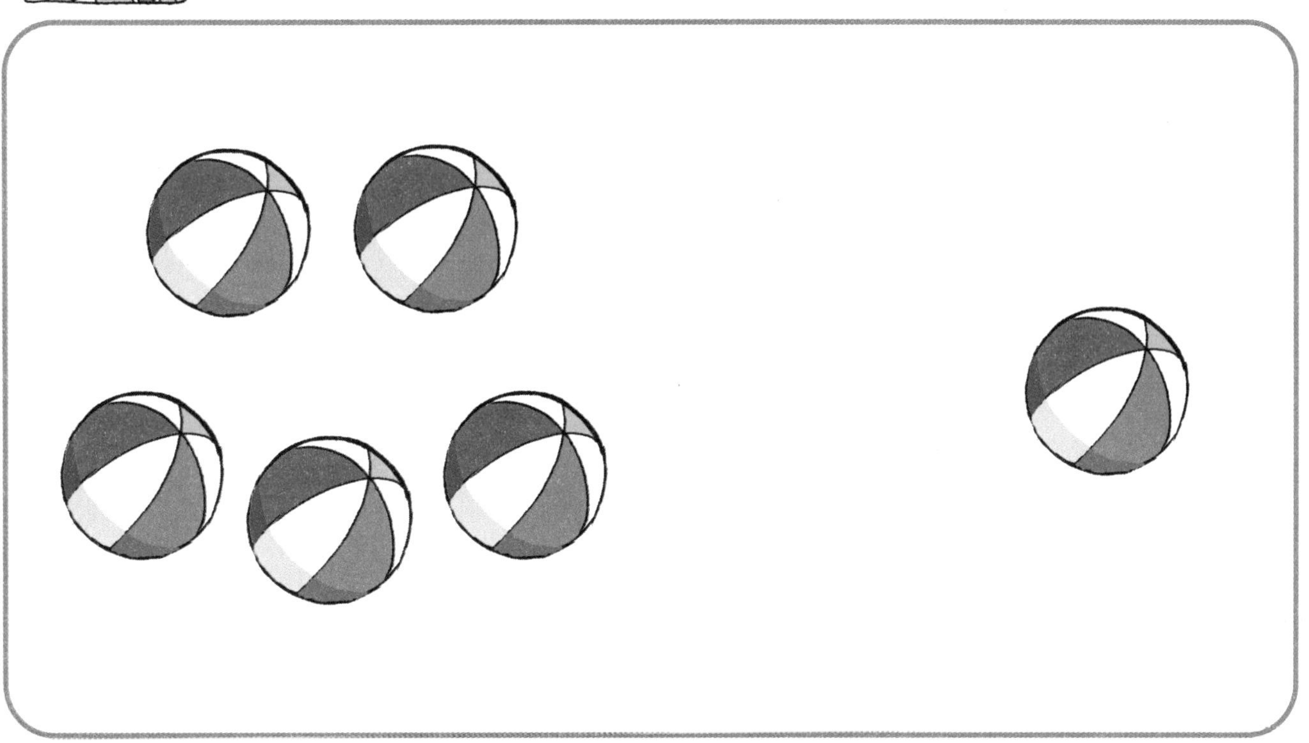

Directions: Circle the group in each box that has **more.**

Larger Number

Name ______________________

8 4	2 6	
7 6	4 9	2 4
9 4	3 7	8 3
5 8	6 9	8 5

Directions: Circle the **larger** number in each box.

Smaller Number

Name ______________________________

1 9	5 8	5 7
9 8	6 9	8 2
5 6	4 7	7 9
1 2	3 9	5 3

Directions: Circle the **smaller** number in each box.

Penny

Name ______________________

1¢ 3¢

5¢ 6¢

7¢ 9¢

Directions: A **penny** is worth 1¢. Circle the correct amount of money in each row above.

Penny

Name ______________________

2¢ 3¢ 

1¢ 2¢ 3¢

4¢ 5¢ 6¢

7¢ 8¢ 9¢

Directions: Circle the correct amount of money in each row above.

Nickel

Name ____________________

5¢

7¢ 9¢

1¢ 5¢

8¢ 10¢

Directions: A **nickel** is worth 5¢ (or five pennies). Circle the correct amount of money in each row above.

Nickel

Name ______________________

8¢ 9¢  10¢

6¢ 7¢ 8¢

10¢ 11¢ 12¢

13¢ 14¢ 15¢

Directions: Circle the correct amount of money in each row above.

Dime

Name

8¢ 9¢ 10¢

11¢ 12¢ 13¢

13¢ 14¢ 15¢

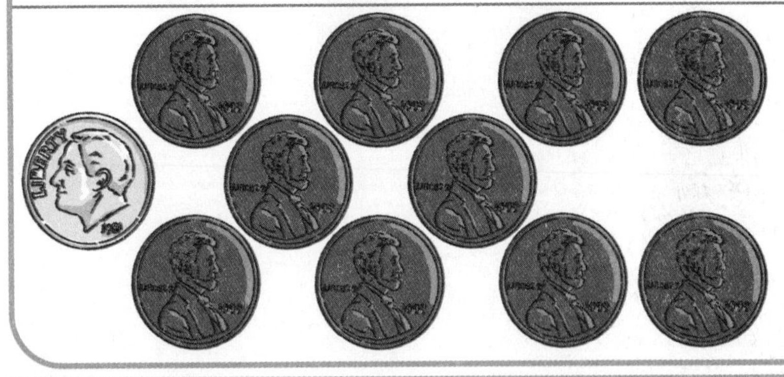

18¢ 19¢ 20¢

Directions: A **dime** is worth 10¢ (or 10 pennies). Circle the correct amount of money in each row above.

Quarter

Name

25¢

Directions: A quarter is worth 25¢. Help Little Critter find all of the things that cost 25¢. Draw an **X** on each one.

Coin Recognition

Name ______________________________

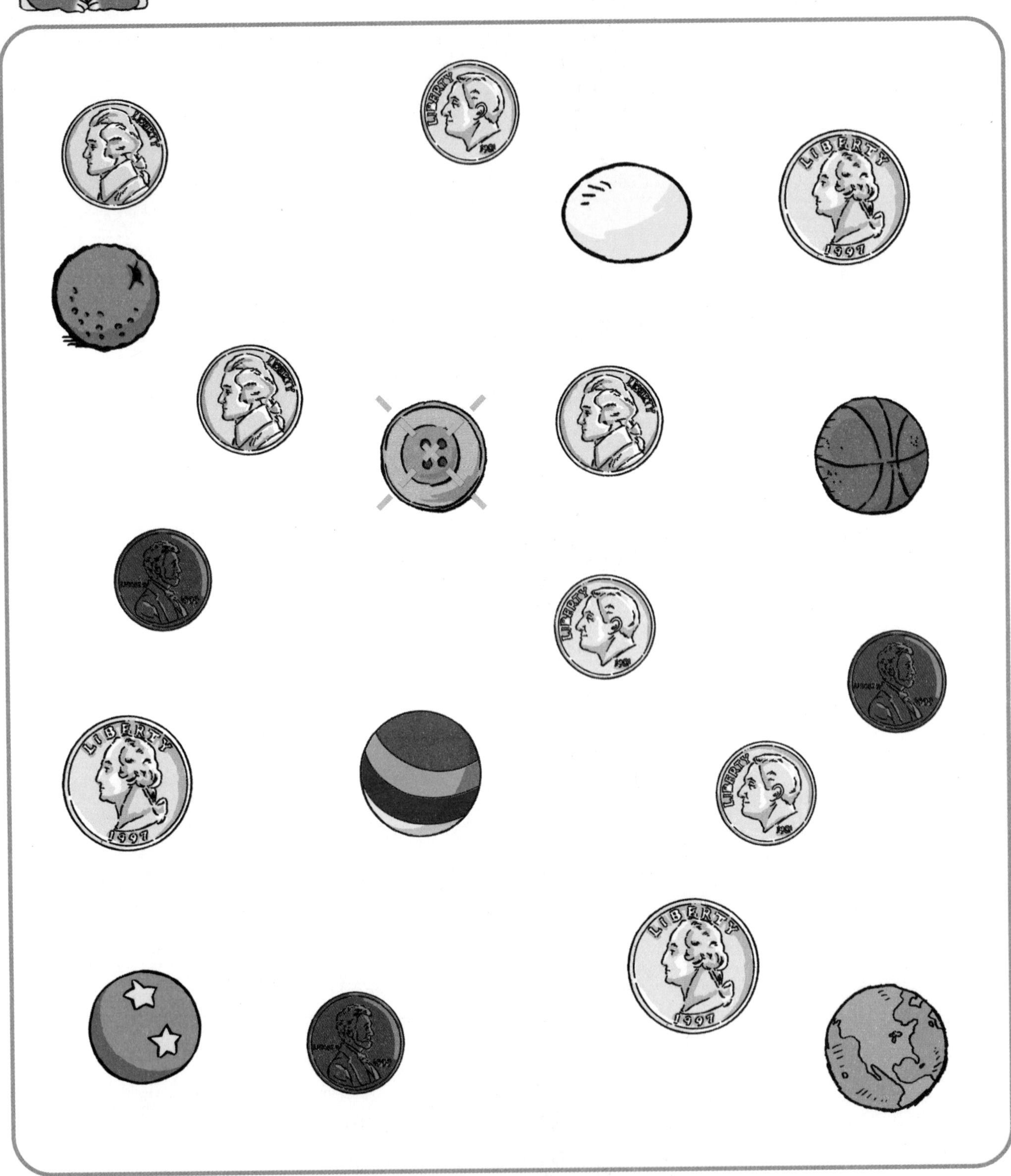

Directions: Cross out each object above that is not a coin.

Sorting Coins

Name

penny

nickel

dime

quarter

Directions: Ask an adult for a handful of change. Sort the coins in the boxes above.
Parent Note: Work with your child to sort the coins. Name the coins. Talk about the presidents found on the coins. Use a magnifying glass to examine each coin more closely.

Days of the Week

Name

Sunday

Monday

Tuesday

Wednesday

Thursday

Friday

Saturday

Parent Note: Post these days of the week on a bulletin board or fridge. Talk about different events that happen on certain days. For example: Monday is the day we go to music. You can draw musical notes beside Monday to give your child something to remind him or her that Monday is music day. Clap while you say the days of the week. Which day of the week has 3 claps?

Time: Counting Clocks

Name ______________________________

Digital Clocks

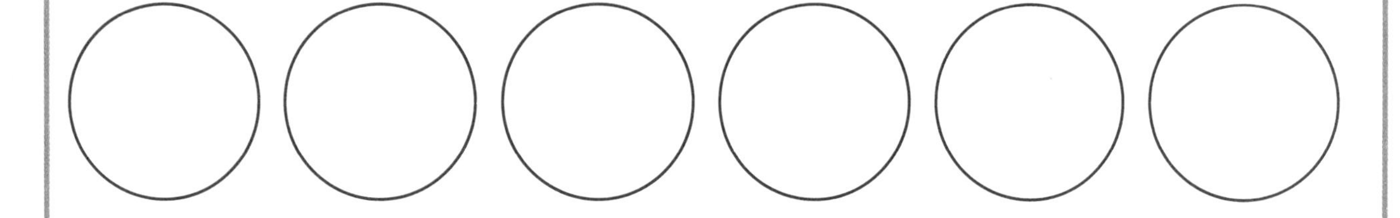

Analog Clocks

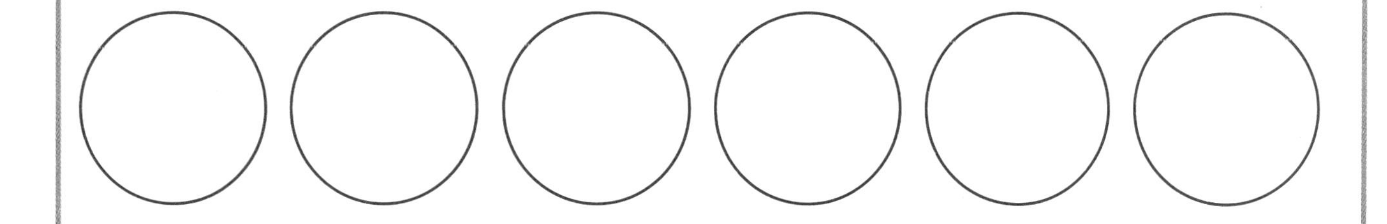

Watches

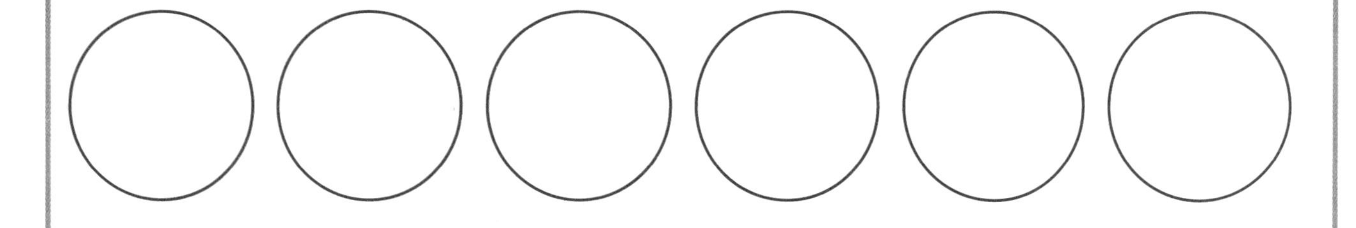

Directions: Count how many clocks and watches there are in your house. Color in one circle for each clock or watch you count.

Time: Numbers on the Clock

Name ______________________

Directions: Trace the numbers 1 to 12 in order on the clock.

Graphing: Sports

Name

soccer ball	soccer ball	soccer ball	soccer ball	soccer ball		4
basketball	basketball	basketball	basketball			
football	football	football				

Directions: This graph shows the different sports the Critterville Kids like. How many Critterville Kids like soccer? Count the filled boxes. Write the number at the end of the row. Do the same for the rest of the sports.

Graphing: Colors

Name

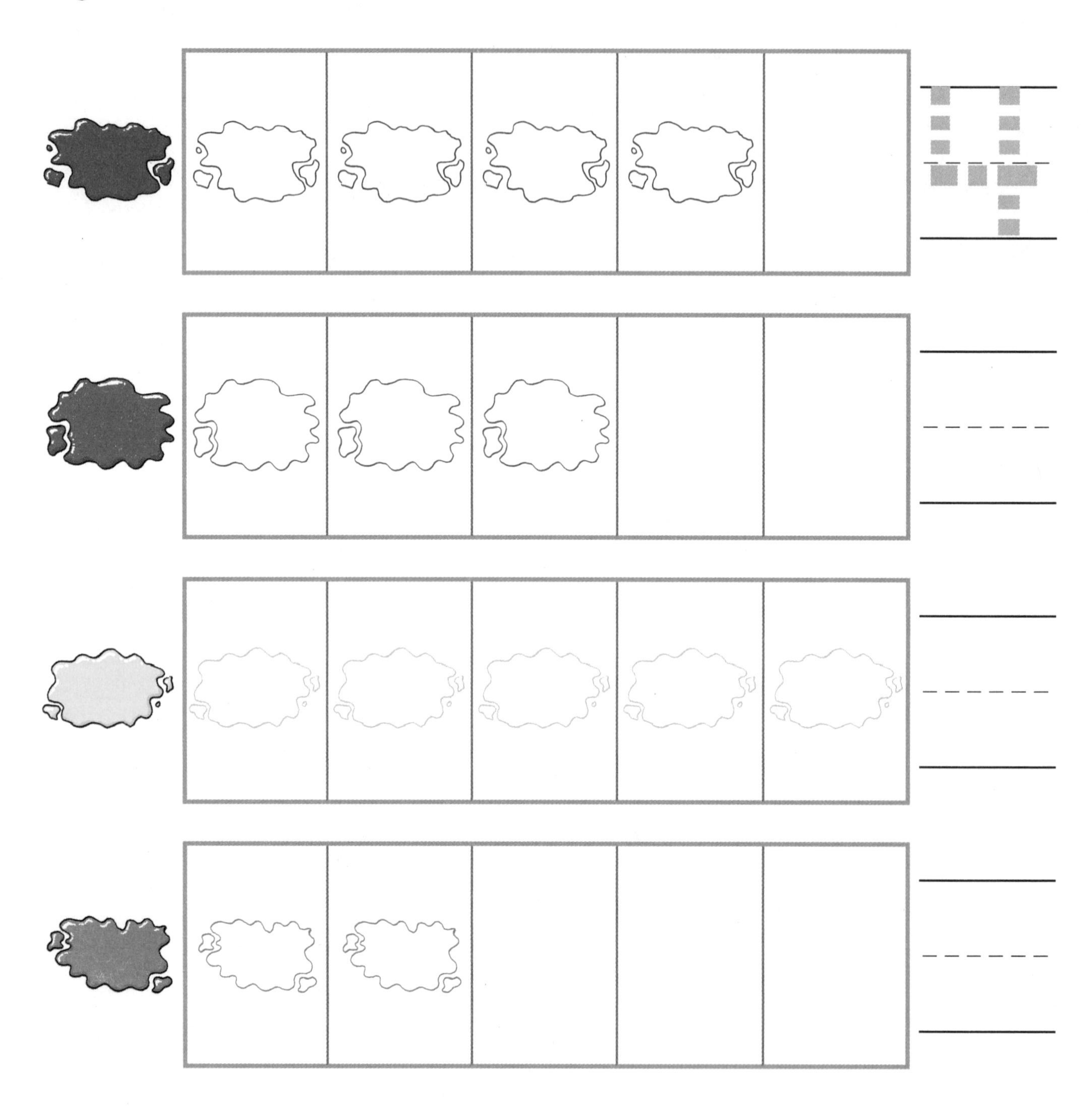

Directions: This graph shows the favorite colors of the Critterville Kids. How many critters like blue? Count the filled boxes. Write the number at the end of the row. Do the same for the rest of the colors.

Graphing: Pets

Name ______________________________

6				
5				
4				
3				
2				
1				

Directions: Help Little Critter count the pets in the window. Then color one box for each animal on the graph above. The first one is done for you.

Graphing: Food

Name ______________________________

10				
9				
8				
7				
6				
5				
4				
3				
2				
1				

hot dog

hamburger

pizza

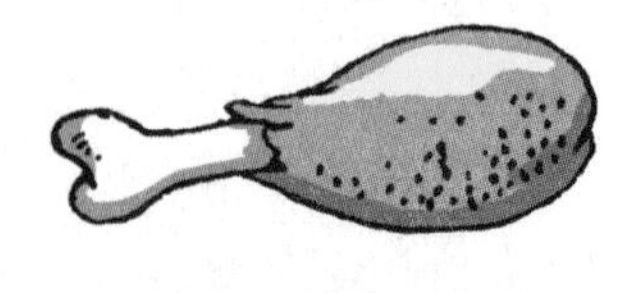

chicken

Directions: Look at the graph above. Then answer the questions on the next page.

Graphing: Food

Name

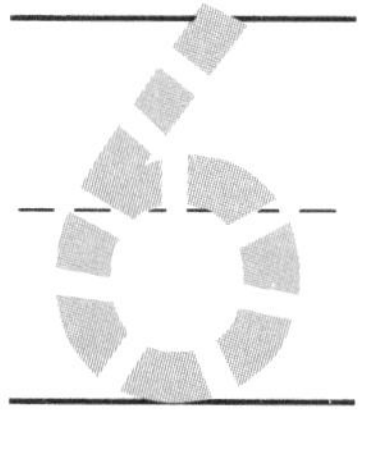

★ How many critters like hot dogs best?

★ How many critters like pizza best?

★ How many critters like chicken best?

★ Circle the food that most critters like best.

hot dog

hamburger

pizza

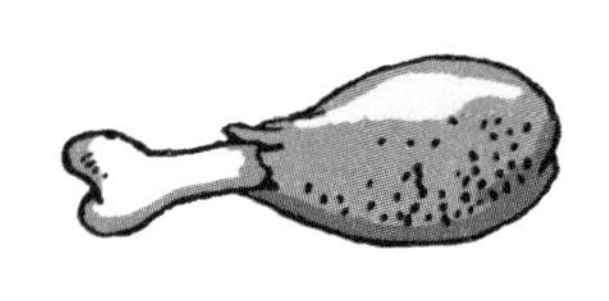

chicken

Directions: Have an adult read the questions above. Then answer the questions about the graph on page 104.

Sequencing: Little Sister

Name

1st

2nd

3rd

Directions: Have an adult carefully tear out page 107 and cut out the pictures. Then, arrange the pictures to show what happened 1st, 2nd, and 3rd. Glue the pictures on this page.

Sequencing: Little Sister

Name

Directions: Have an adult carefully tear out this page and cut out the pictures. Put the pictures in order and then glue them on page 106.

This page is blank for the cutting activity on the opposite side of the page.

Sequencing: Dad

Name

Directions: Have an adult carefully tear out this page and cut out the pictures. Put the pictures in order and then glue them on page 111.

This page is blank for the
cutting activity on the opposite side
of the page.

Sequencing: Dad

Name

1st

2nd

3rd

Directions: Have an adult carefully tear out page 109 and cut out the pictures. Then, arrange the pictures to show what happened 1st, 2nd, and 3rd. Glue the pictures on this page.

Sequencing: Gabby

Name

1st

2nd

3rd

Directions: Have an adult carefully tear out page 113 and cut out the pictures. Then, arrange the pictures to show what happened 1st, 2nd, and 3rd. Glue the pictures on this page.

Sequencing: Gabby

Name

Directions: Have an adult carefully tear out this page and cut out the pictures. Put the pictures in order and then glue them on page 112.

This page is blank for the
cutting activity on the opposite side
of the page.

Sequencing: Little Critter and Blue

Name

Directions: Write a number in each box to show the correct order in which to tell the story.

Sequencing: Snowcritter

Name ________________

1st

2nd

3rd

4th

Directions: Have an adult carefully tear out page 117 and cut out the pictures. Then, arrange the pictures to show what happened 1st, 2nd, and 3rd. Draw your own picture to show what happened next. Finally, glue the pictures on this page.

Sequencing: Snowcritter

Name

Directions: Have an adult carefully tear out this page and cut out the pictures. Put the pictures in order. Draw what you think will happen next. Then glue the pictures on page 116.

This page is blank for the
cutting activity on the opposite side
of the page.

Thinking Skills

Name

- The house is white.
- The house has a red door.
- The house has a fence in front of it.

Directions: Read the clues above. Draw an **X** on each house that does not fit the clues. Circle the correct house.

Thinking Skills

Name

- The mitten is green.
- The mitten has two different shapes on it.
- The mitten has hearts on it.

Directions: Read the clues above. Draw an **X** on each mitten that does not fit the clues. Circle the correct mitten.

Number Concentration

Name

Directions: Have an adult cut out the cards from this page and page 123. Lay the cards facedown. Turn two cards faceup. If the cards match, take the cards. If they do not match, turn the cards facedown. Take turns with a friend. Have fun!

Number Concentration

Name

Directions: Have an adult cut out the cards from this page and page 121. Lay the cards facedown. Turn two cards faceup. If the cards match, take the cards. If they do not match, turn the cards facedown. Take turns with a friend. Have fun!

Practice Page

Name

Use this page for extra practice.

Practice Page

Name

Use this page for extra practice.

Practice Page

Name

Use this page for extra practice.

Math to Try at Home

- Encourage your child to find numbers around the house (clocks, television, telephone, etc.) and tell you how they are used.

- Look for and read numbers as you ride in the car: street signs, house numbers, at gas stations and other businesses, license plate numbers, etc.

- Tell your child how you use numbers in your job and at home.

- Look for numbers in the grocery store. Have your child help you find the prices of items.

- Label different household items with "prices" and play store with your child.

- Bumpy Numbers: Put drops of glue on index cards. After the glue dries have your child close his or her eyes and try to feel the number of dots.

- Capitalize on everyday opportunities to count with your child and to have him or her practice counting. Count cans in the cupboard as you put them away. Count books on the bookshelf or toys as they are picked up.

Math to Try at Home

- Have your child listen and identify the number of times that you make a special noise like clapping or snapping your fingers.

- Let your child play counting and number games with blocks. For example, count how many blocks tall you can make a tower before it topples!

- Make number cards with index cards. Write a number from 1 to 20 on each card and have your child practice putting the cards in order.

- Give your child a number card and a supply of small objects (macaroni, beads, blocks, etc.) and have him or her practice counting the correct number of objects. Let your child practice with many different numbers. Then count out a number of objects and have your child match the correct number card to it.

- Say a number and have your child tell you what number comes after it or before it.

- Use magazine pictures to make a counting book. Write a number on each page and have your child cut out pictures of that number of objects on the page.

- Find numbers in catalogs and let your child practice reading them.

Math to Try at Home

- Punch ten holes in an old greeting card cover with a nice picture. Number the holes. Give your child a piece of string and have him or her thread the holes in the correct order.

- Sing "This Old Man" with your child, having him or her use fingers to represent numbers.

- Use the calendar to help your child with number recognition. Talk with your child about the date and month and count the number of days until a special event.

- Place different numbers of objects in an egg carton to give your child practice counting numbers to 12.

- Number clothespins from 1 to 12. Label index cards with the number of words on one side and the corresponding number of dots on the other side. Play a game with your child, having him or her clip the clothespins on the correct card.

Math to Try at Home

- Challenge your child to count back from 10.
- Have your child shape clay into each of the numbers from 1 to 20.
- Draw a number on your child's back with your finger. Have your child tell you what number you drew. Then let your child draw a number on your back.
- Talk with your child about ways he or she helps at home. Ask: How can learning to count help us in setting the table?
- Have your child help set the table. Help him or her use one napkin for each plate, one fork for each napkin, etc.
- Cook with your child. Have him or her help measure ingredients, stir for a certain number of minutes, set timers, and eat!
- Put out a small pile of coins and have your child practice sorting and naming them. Have pennies, nickels, dimes, and quarters available for your child to manipulate. Have your child count how many there are of each coin and talk about the value of each coin.

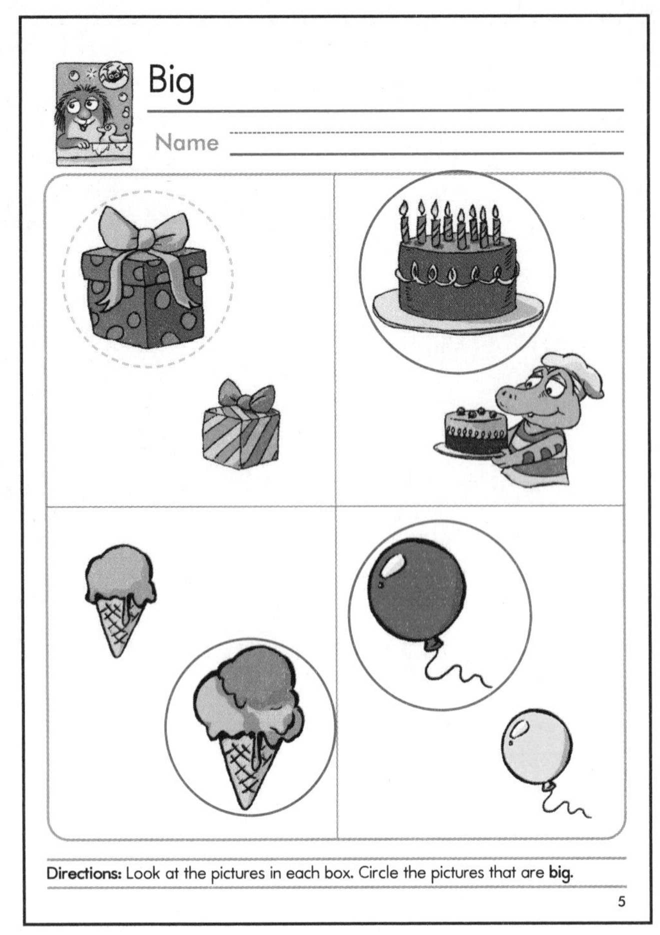
Big
Name
Directions: Look at the pictures in each box. Circle the pictures that are big.
5

Small
Name
Directions: Look at the pictures in each box. Circle the pictures that are small.
6

Smallest to Biggest
Name
2nd
3rd
1st
4th
Directions: Have an adult cut out the boxes above. Then, on another sheet of paper, line up Little Critter's pets in order from smallest to biggest.
7

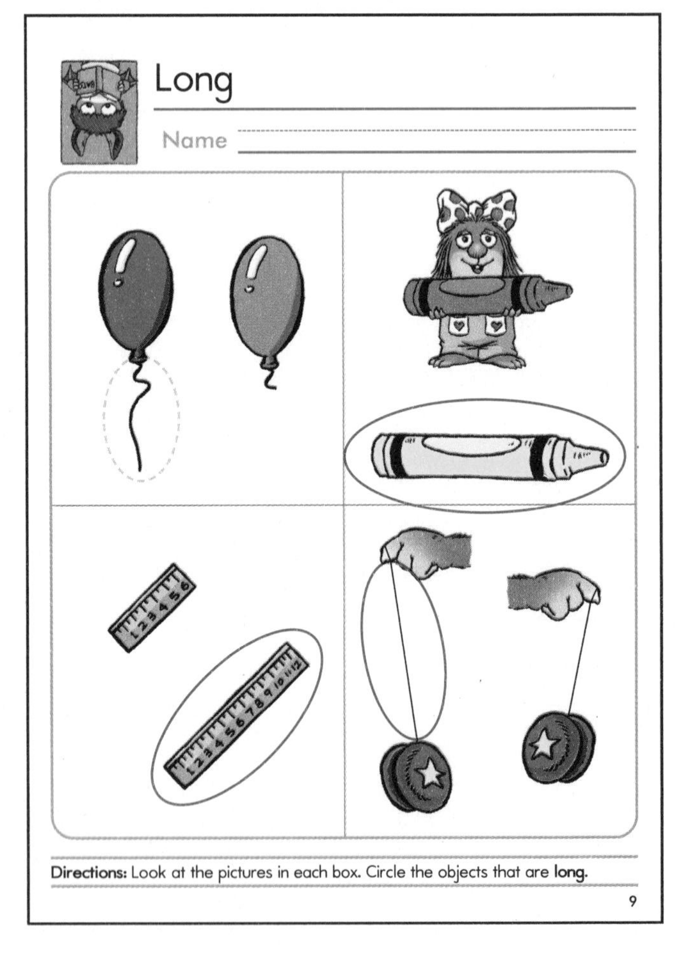
Long
Name
Directions: Look at the pictures in each box. Circle the objects that are long.
9

Short

Name

Directions: Look at the pictures in each box. Circle the pictures that are **short.**

10

Tall

Name

Directions: Look at the pictures in each box. Circle the pictures that are **tall.**

11

Full

Name

Directions: Look at the pictures in each box. Circle the containers that are **full.**

12

Empty

Name

Directions: Look at the pictures in each box. Circle the containers that are **empty.**

13

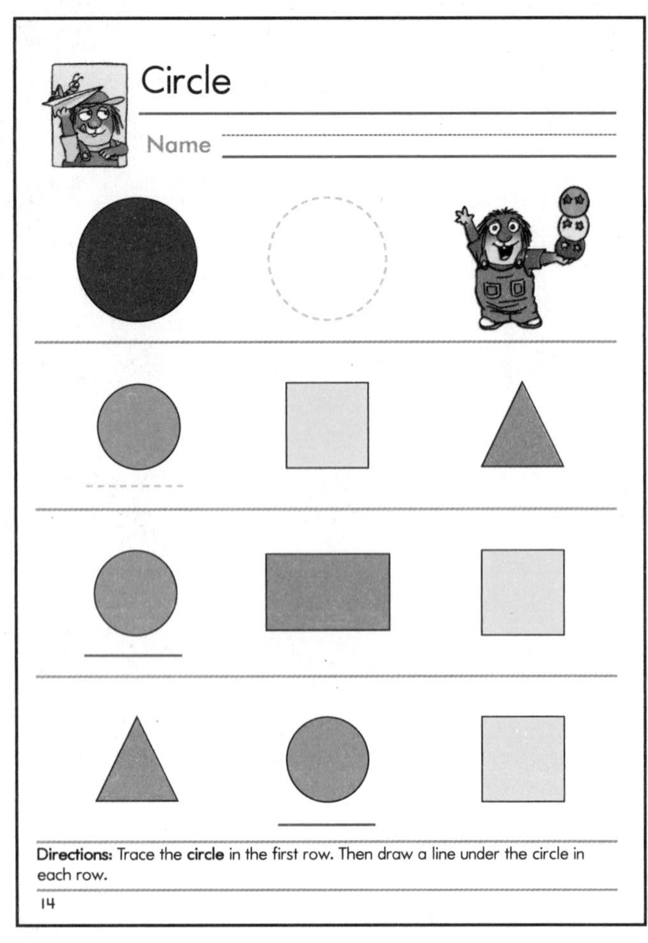

Circle

Name

Directions: Trace the **circle** in the first row. Then draw a line under the circle in each row.

14

Find the Circles

Name

Directions: Tiger is fast asleep. Look at the objects in his room. Draw an **X** on each object that has the shape of a **circle.**

15

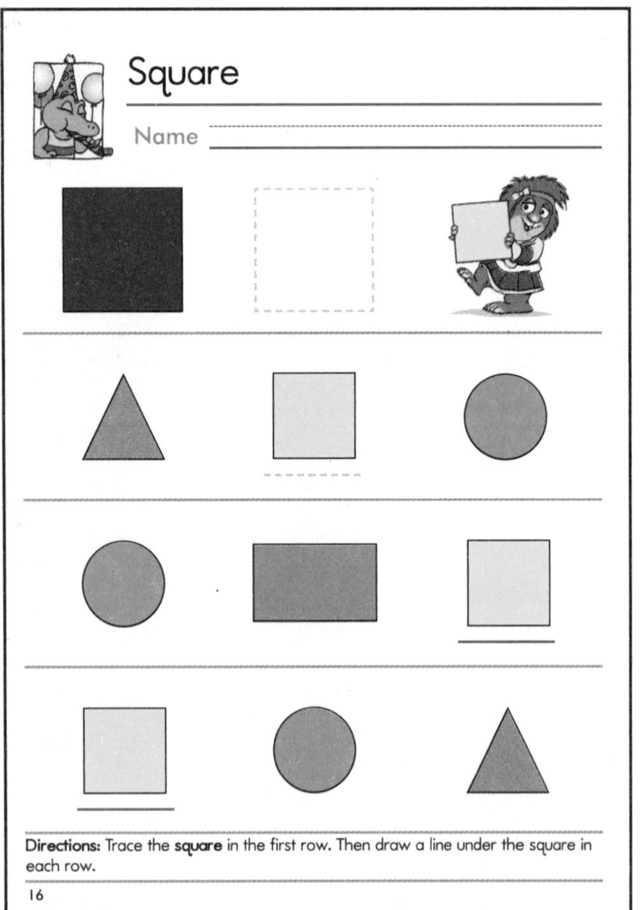

Square

Name

Directions: Trace the **square** in the first row. Then draw a line under the square in each row.

16

Find the Squares

Name

Directions: Gator and Bat Child are having a snack. Look at the objects in Gator's room. Draw an **X** on each object that has the shape of a **square.**

17

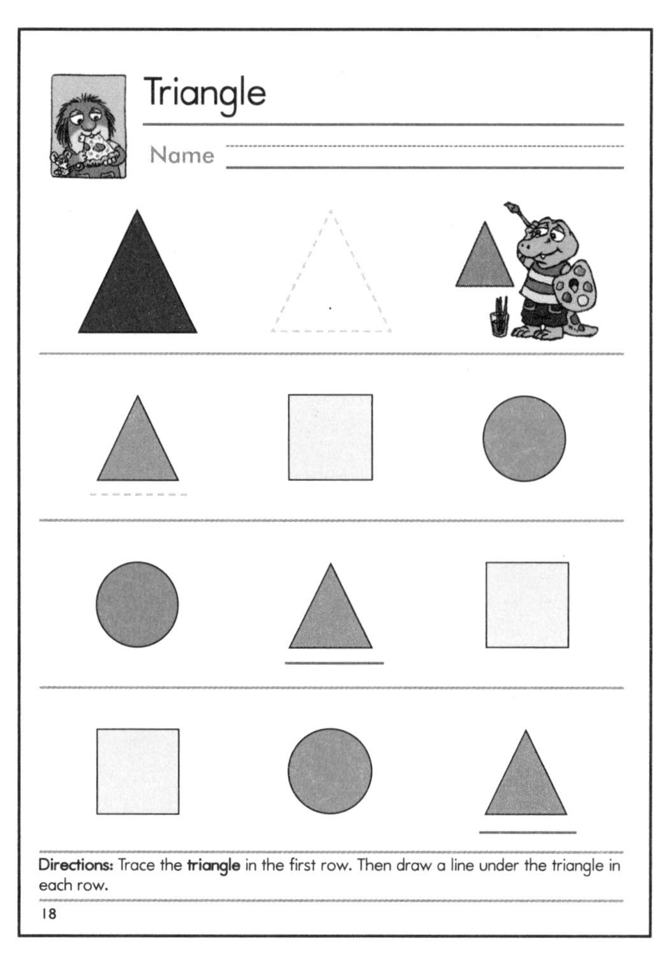

Triangle

Name

Directions: Trace the **triangle** in the first row. Then draw a line under the triangle in each row.

18

Find the Triangles

Name

Directions: Malcolm is camping. Look at Malcolm's campsite. Draw an **X** on each object that has the shape of a **triangle**.

19

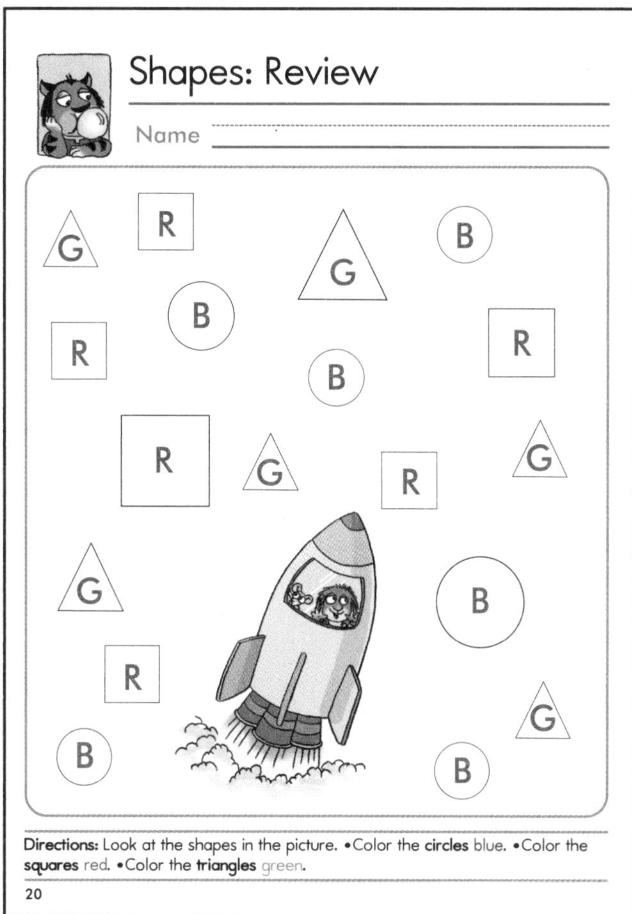

Shapes: Review

Name

Directions: Look at the shapes in the picture. •Color the **circles** blue. •Color the **squares** red. •Color the **triangles** green.

20

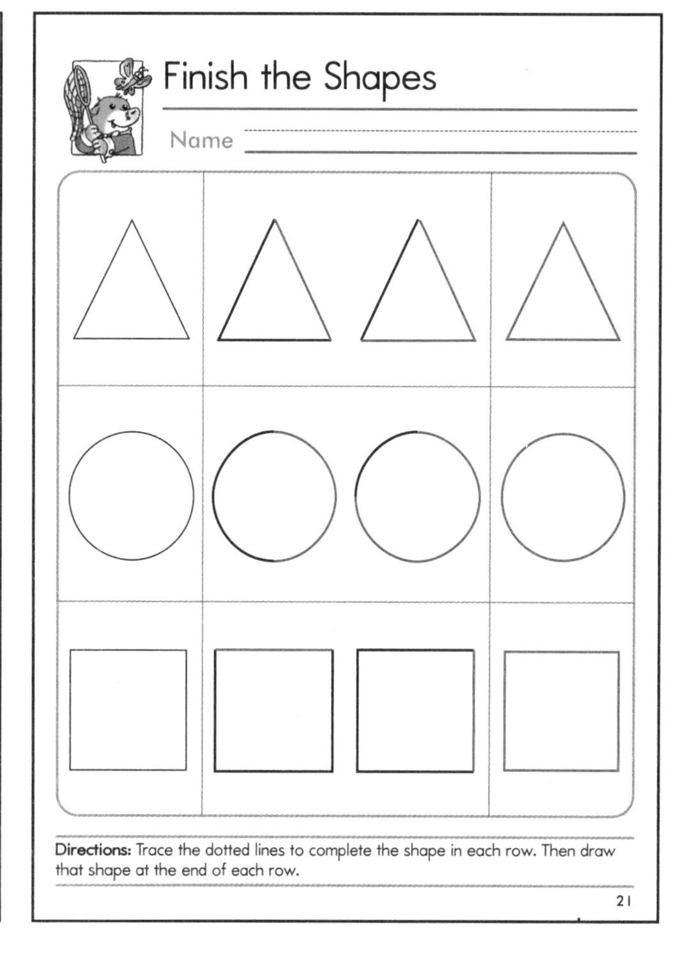

Finish the Shapes

Name

Directions: Trace the dotted lines to complete the shape in each row. Then draw that shape at the end of each row.

21

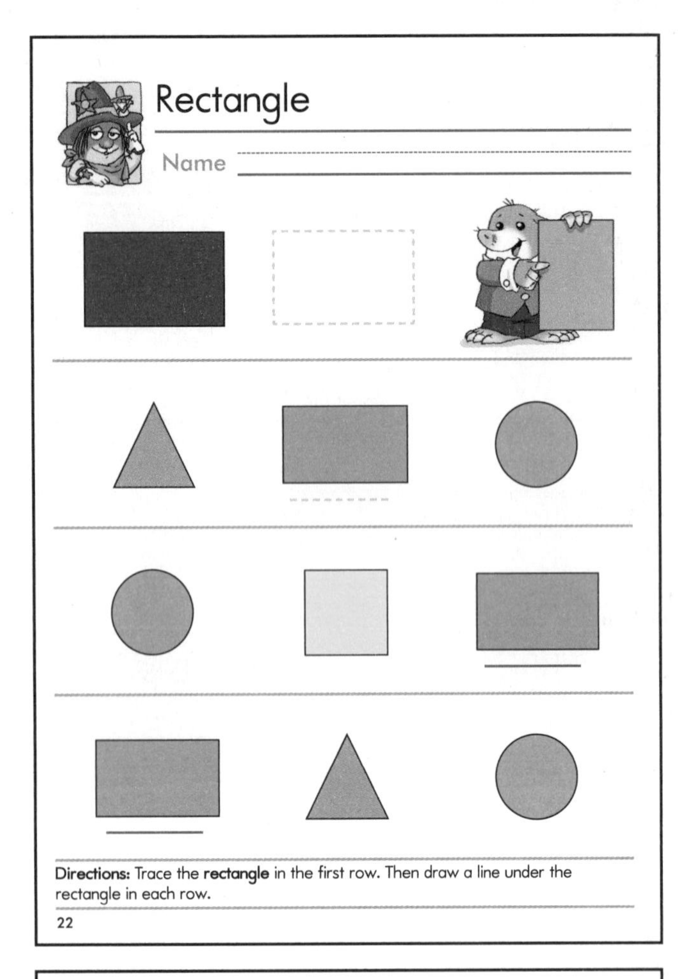

Rectangle

Name

Directions: Trace the **rectangle** in the first row. Then draw a line under the rectangle in each row.

22

Finding the Rectangles

Name

Directions: It's Bun Bun's birthday. Look at the objects at her party. Draw an X on each object that has the shape of a **rectangle**.

23

Shapes: Review

Name

Directions: Little Critter is taking a bath. Look at the objects in the picture. •Color the **circle**. •Draw a line from the **rectangle** to Little Critter. •Draw an X on the **squares**. •Draw a line under the **triangle**.

24

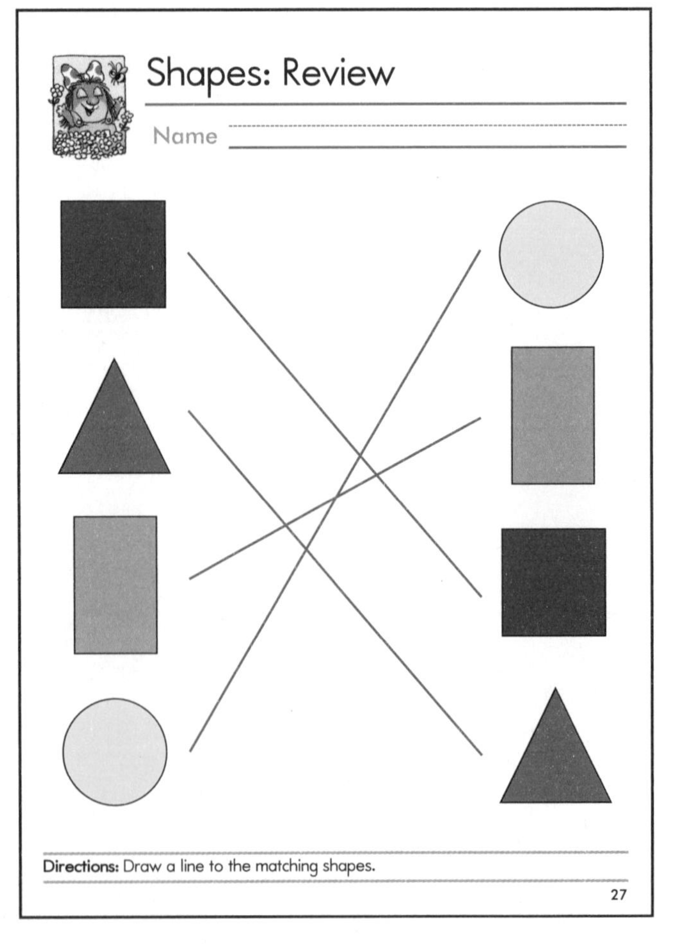

Shapes: Review

Name

Directions: Draw a line to the matching shapes.

27

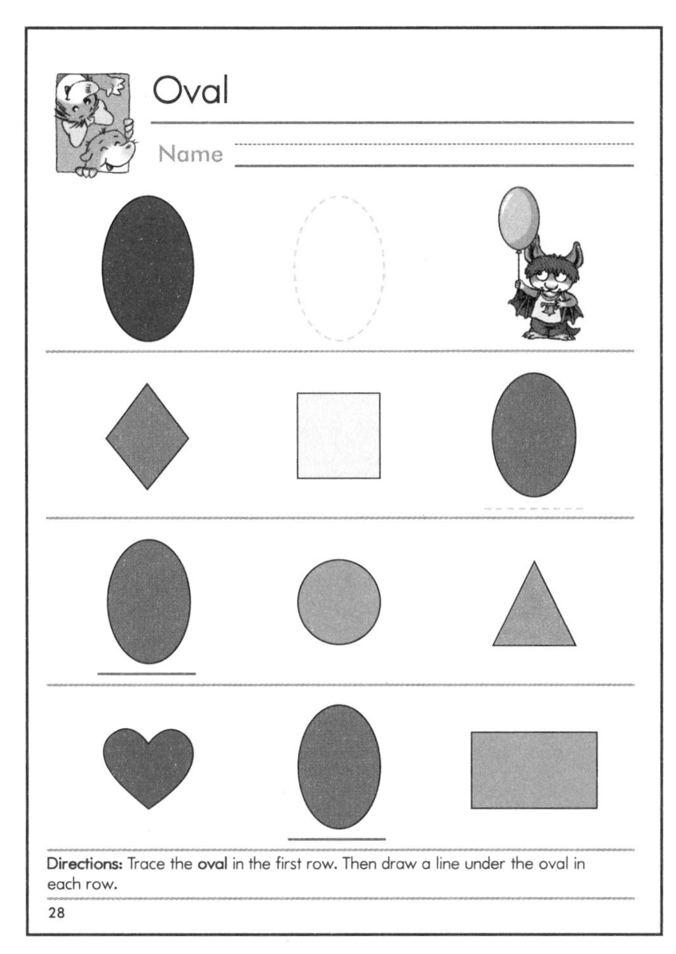

Oval

Name

Directions: Trace the **oval** in the first row. Then draw a line under the oval in each row.

28

Find the Ovals

Name

Directions: Little Sister is in the backyard. Look at the objects around her. Draw an **X** on each object that has the shape of an **oval**.

29

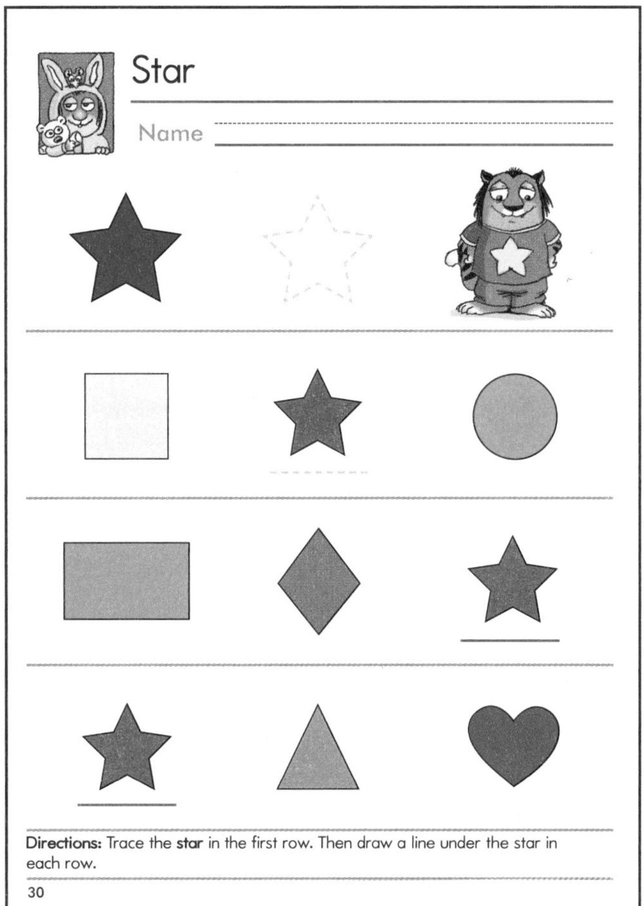

Star

Name

Directions: Trace the **star** in the first row. Then draw a line under the star in each row.

30

Find the Stars

Name

Directions: Maurice is looking for **stars.** Help him find them. Color all the stars blue.

31

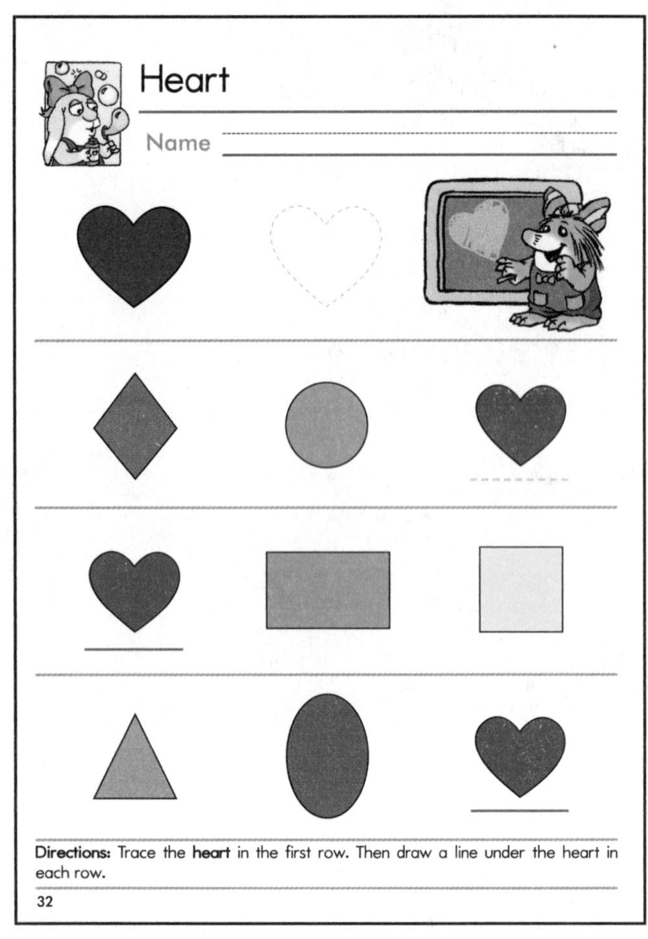
Heart
Name
Directions: Trace the heart in the first row. Then draw a line under the heart in each row.
32

Find the Hearts
Name
TODAY
Directions: It's Valentine's Day in Critterville. Draw an X on each heart in the picture above.
33

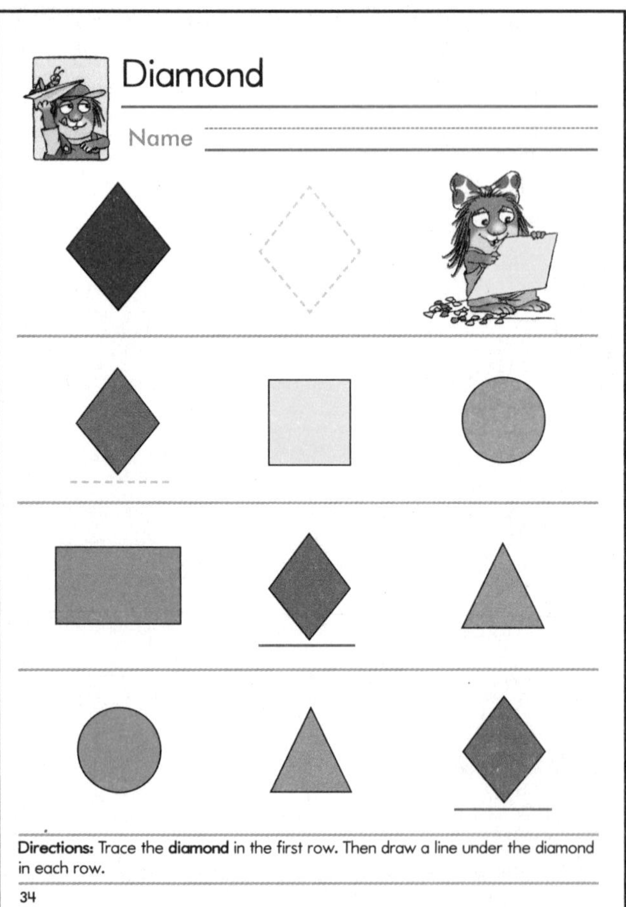
Diamond
Name
Directions: Trace the diamond in the first row. Then draw a line under the diamond in each row.
34

Find the Diamonds
Name
Directions: Maurice, Molly, and Bun Bun are flying kites. Draw an X on each object that has the shape of a diamond.
35

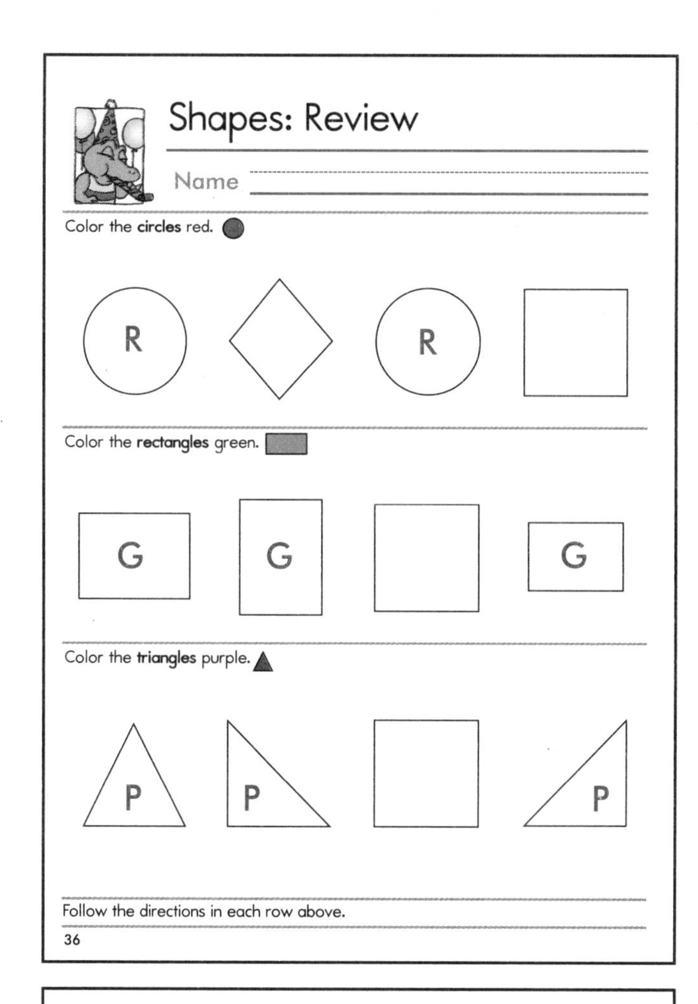

Shapes: Review

Name

Color the **circles** red.

R R

Color the **rectangles** green.

G G G

Color the **triangles** purple.

P P P

Follow the directions in each row above.

36

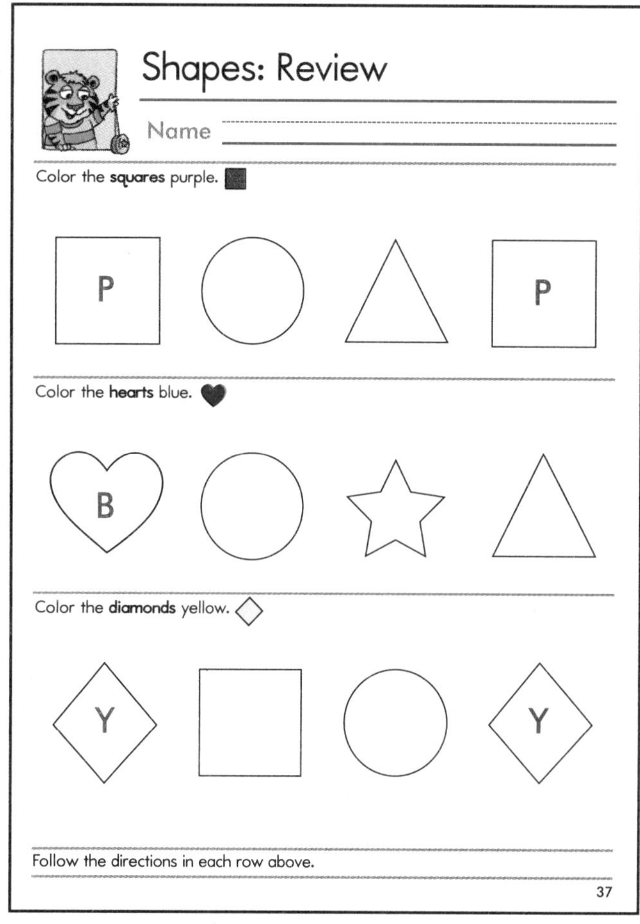

Shapes: Review

Name

Color the **squares** purple.

P P

Color the **hearts** blue.

B

Color the **diamonds** yellow.

Y Y

Follow the directions in each row above.

37

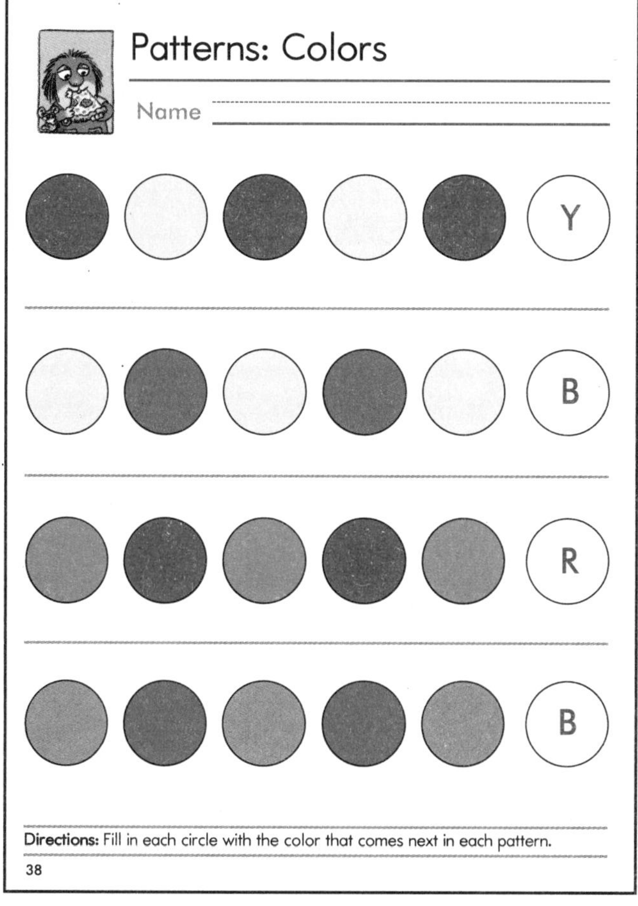

Patterns: Colors

Name

Y

B

R

B

Directions: Fill in each circle with the color that comes next in each pattern.

38

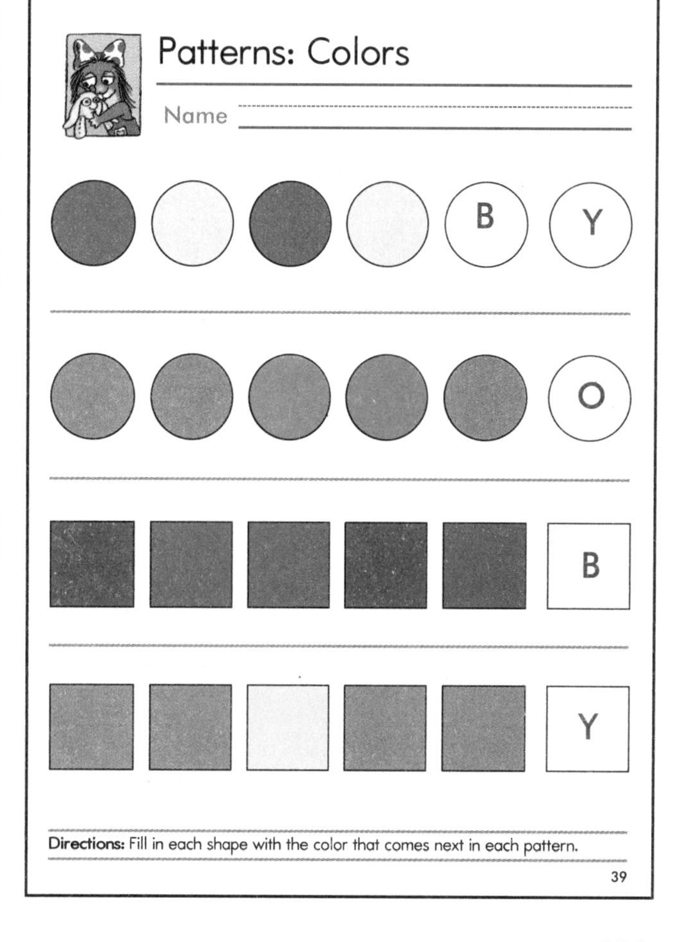

Patterns: Colors

Name

B Y

O

B

Y

Directions: Fill in each shape with the color that comes next in each pattern.

39

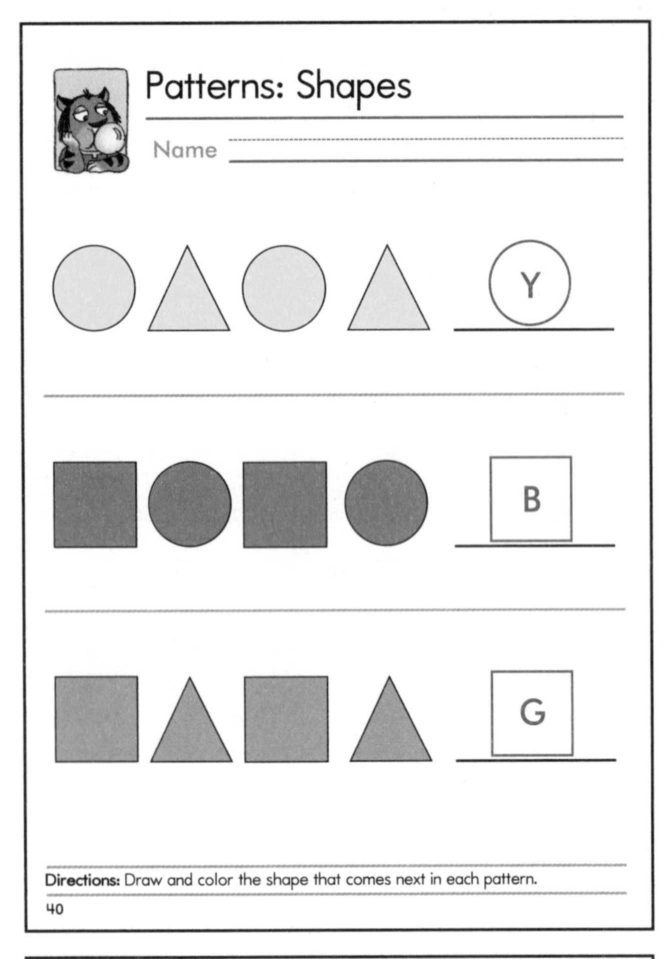
Patterns: Shapes
Name
Y
B
G
Directions: Draw and color the shape that comes next in each pattern.
40

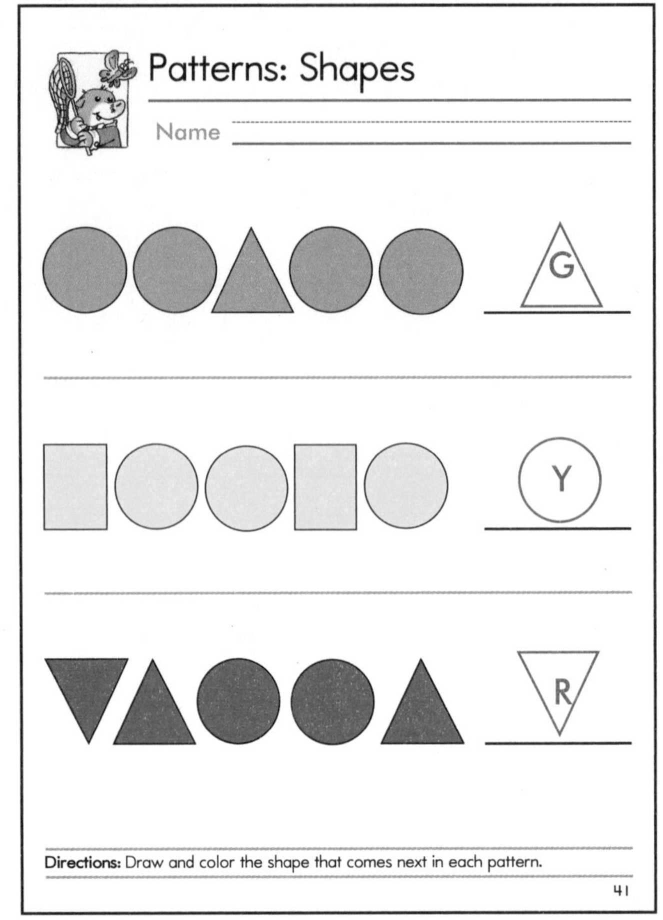
Patterns: Shapes
Name
G
Y
R
Directions: Draw and color the shape that comes next in each pattern.
41

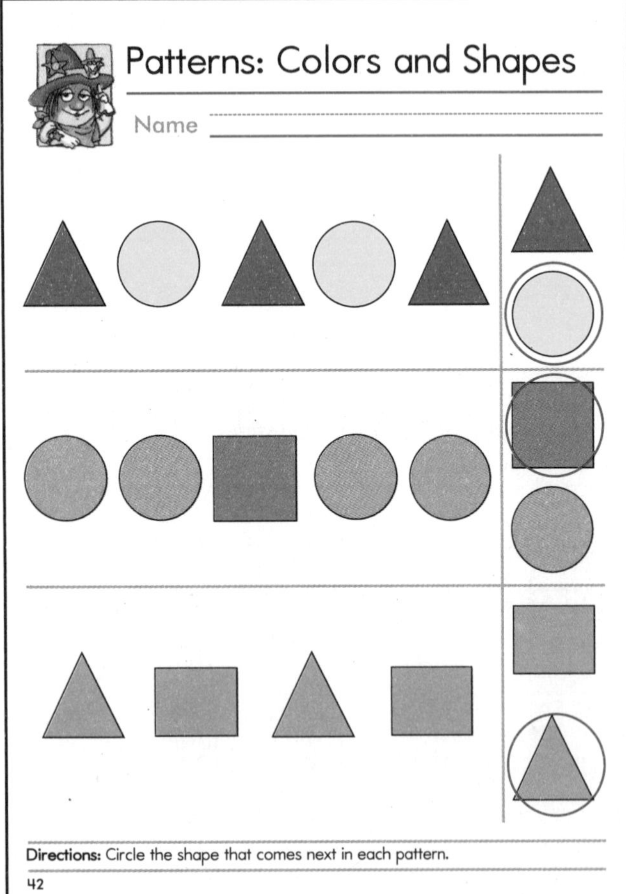
Patterns: Colors and Shapes
Name
Directions: Circle the shape that comes next in each pattern.
42

Patterns: Little Critter and Friends
Name
Answers will vary.
Directions: Have an adult carefully tear out page 43 and cut out the pictures. Then, arrange the pictures in different patterns. Glue some of your patterns to this page.
45

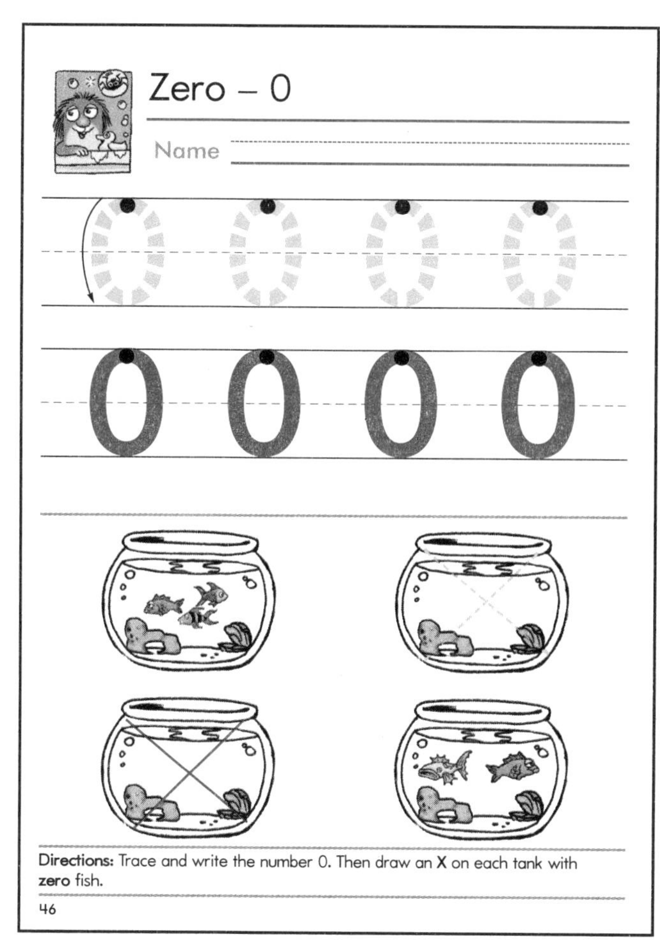
Zero – 0
Name
Directions: Trace and write the number 0. Then draw an X on each tank with zero fish.
46

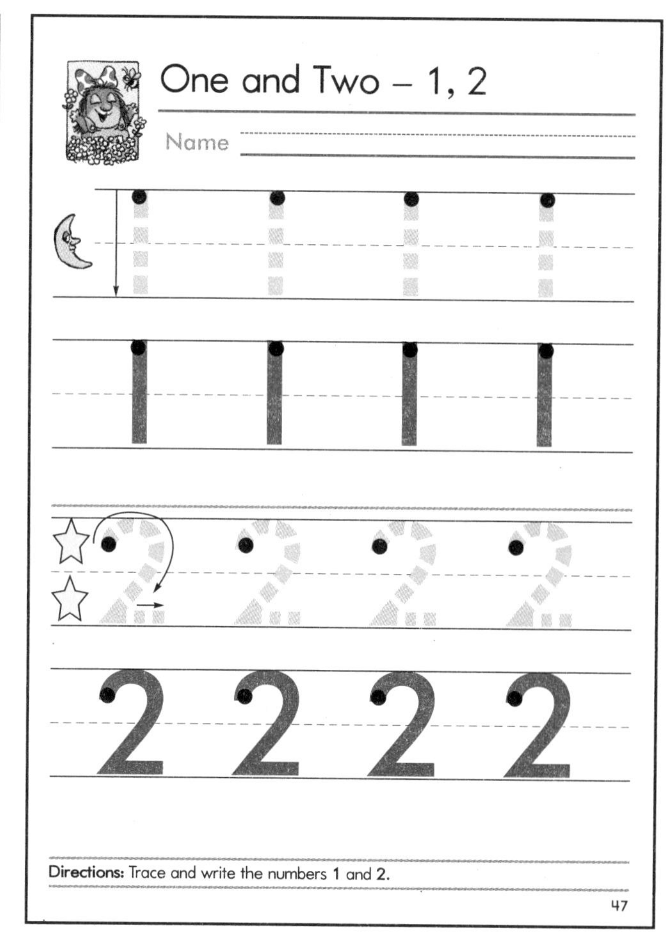
One and Two – 1, 2
Name
Directions: Trace and write the numbers 1 and 2.
47

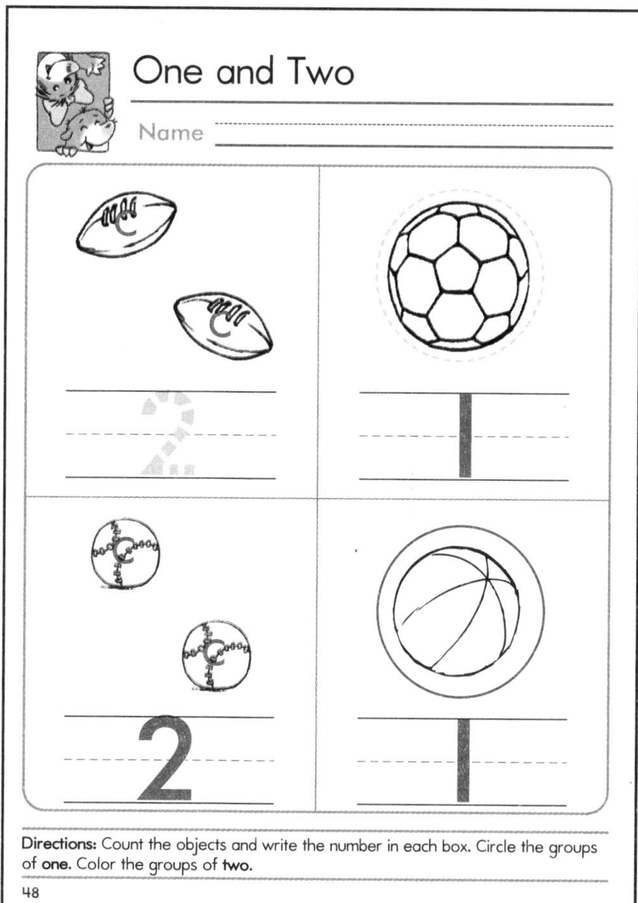
One and Two
Name
Directions: Count the objects and write the number in each box. Circle the groups of one. Color the groups of two.
48

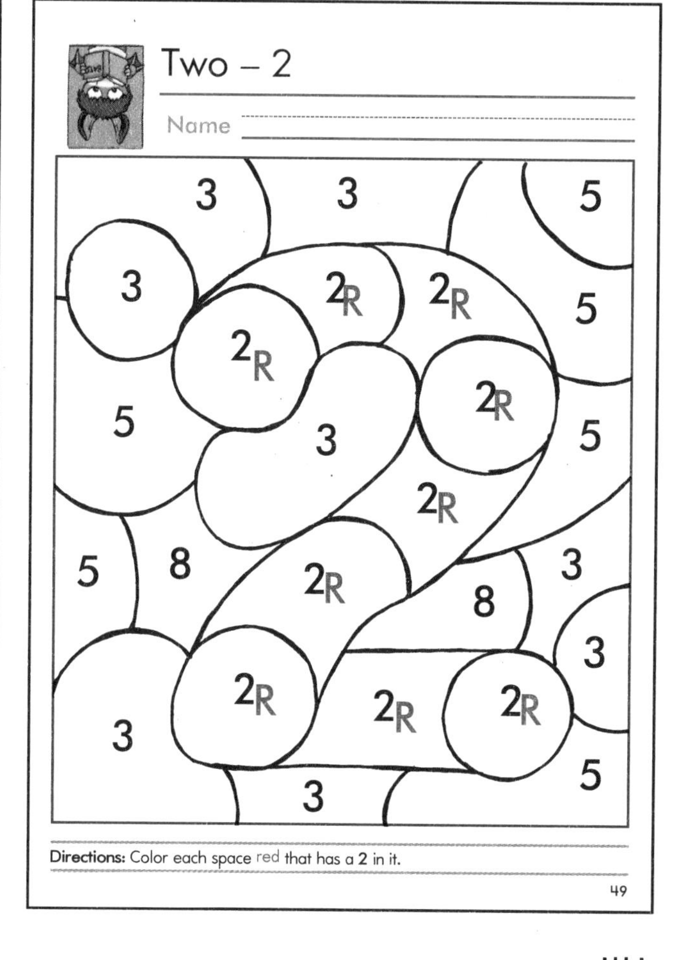
Two – 2
Name
Directions: Color each space red that has a 2 in it.
49

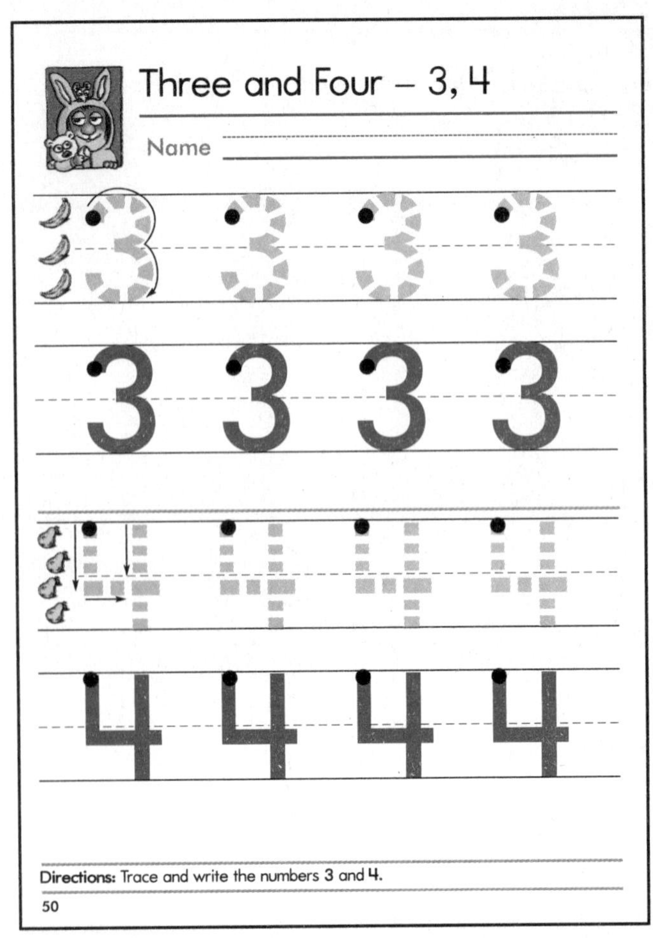

Three and Four – 3, 4

Name

Directions: Trace and write the numbers 3 and 4.

50

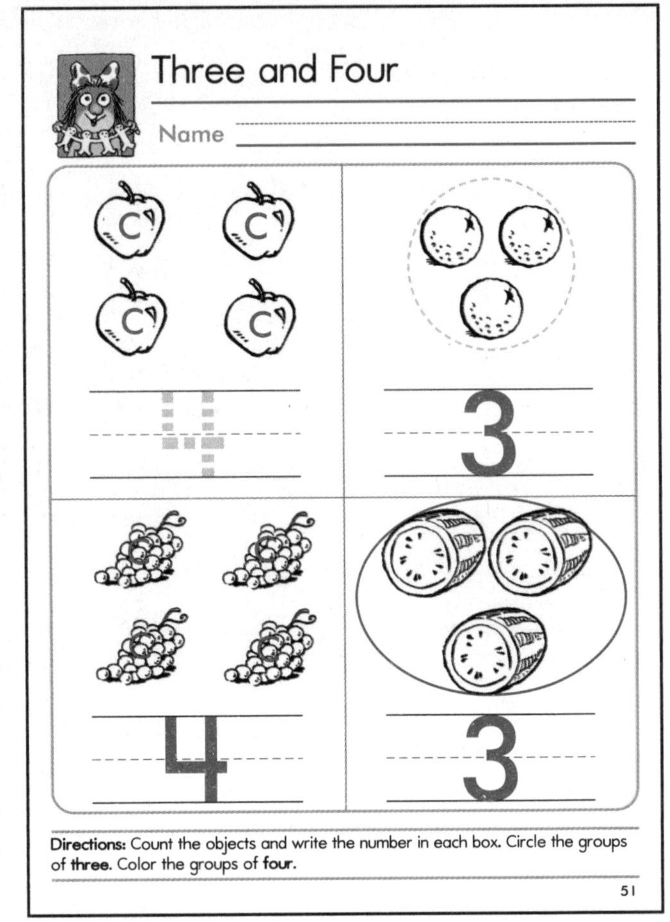

Three and Four

Name

Directions: Count the objects and write the number in each box. Circle the groups of **three**. Color the groups of **four**.

51

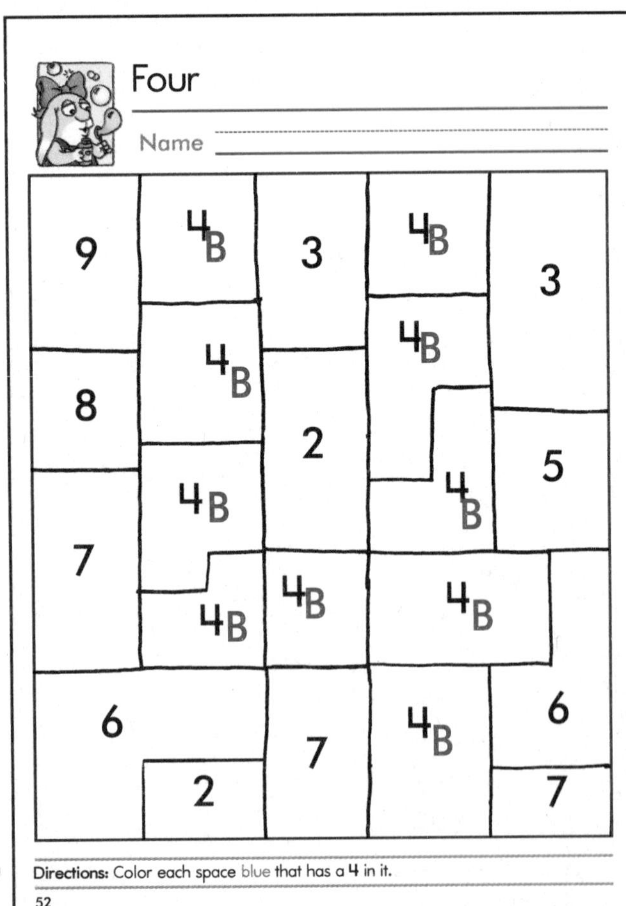

Four

Name

Directions: Color each space blue that has a 4 in it.

52

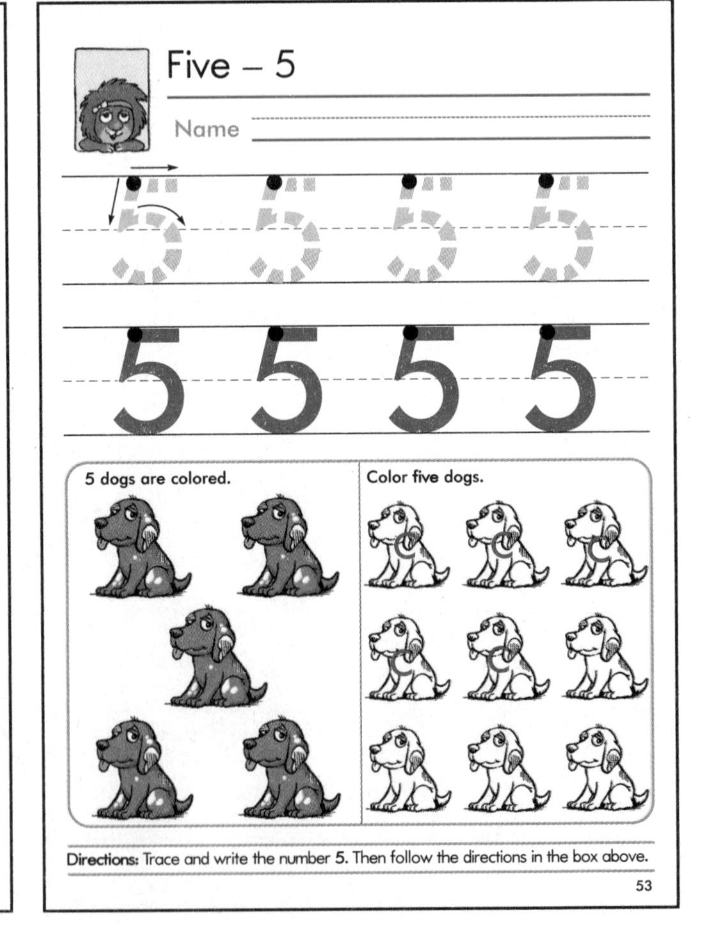

Five – 5

Name

5 dogs are colored.

Color five dogs.

Directions: Trace and write the number **5**. Then follow the directions in the box above.

53

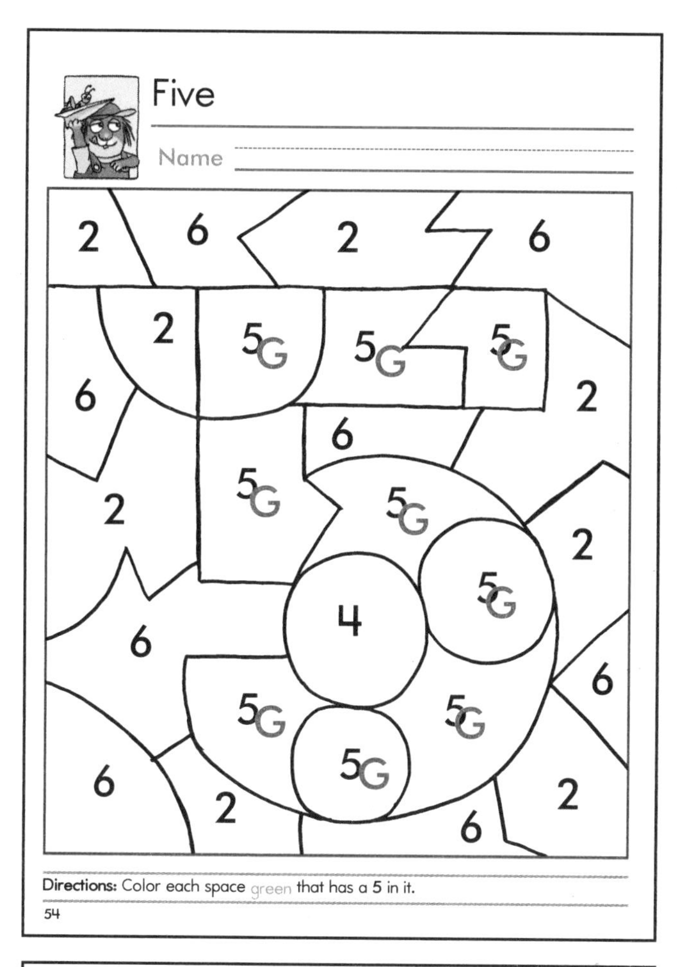

Five

Name

2 6 2 6
2 5G 5G 5G
6 2
6
5G 2 5G 2
4 5G 6
5G 5G 6
5G 2 6 2

Directions: Color each space green that has a 5 in it.

54

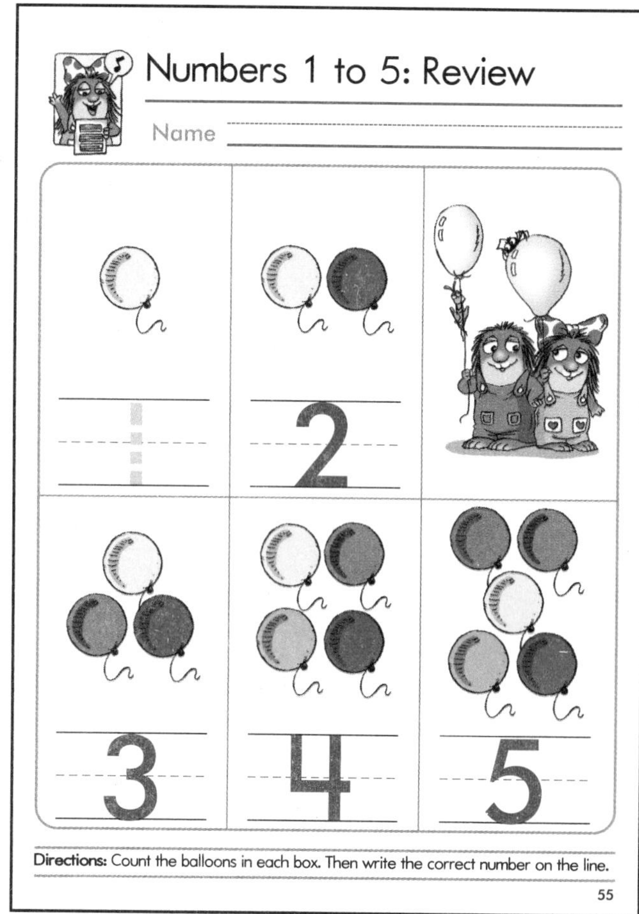

Numbers 1 to 5: Review

Name

1 2

3 4 5

Directions: Count the balloons in each box. Then write the correct number on the line.

55

Dot-to-Dot 1 to 5

Name

Directions: Connect the dots from 1 to 5 to find out where Little Critter and Little Sister are spending the night. Color the picture.

56

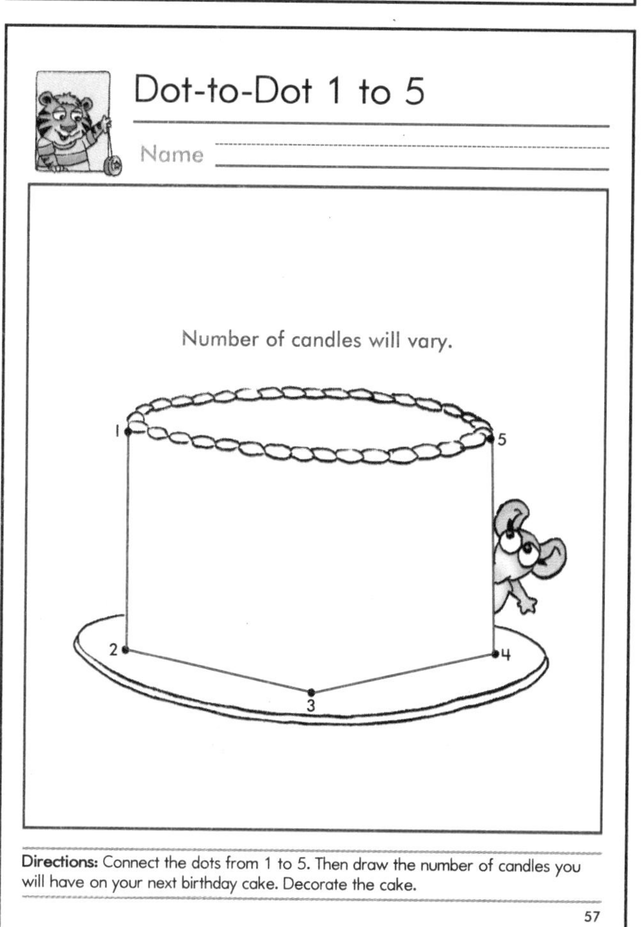

Dot-to-Dot 1 to 5

Name

Number of candles will vary.

Directions: Connect the dots from 1 to 5. Then draw the number of candles you will have on your next birthday cake. Decorate the cake.

57

Six – 6
Name
Directions: Trace and write the number 6. Then draw six coins in the piggy bank.
58

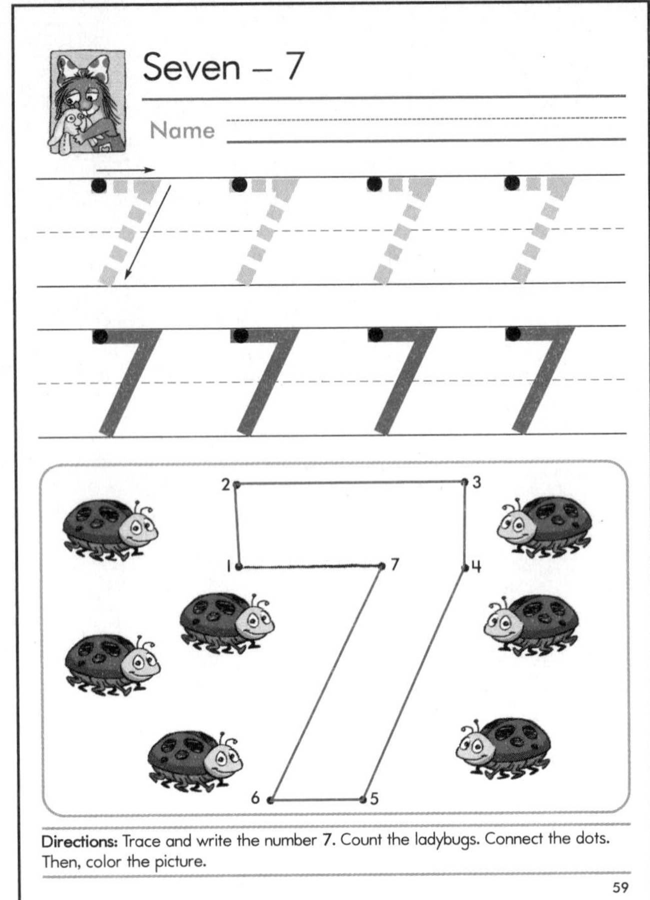
Seven – 7
Name
1
2
3
4
5
6
7
Directions: Trace and write the number 7. Count the ladybugs. Connect the dots. Then, color the picture.
59

Dot-to-Dot 1 to 7
Name
1
2
3
4
5
6
7
BLUE
YUMMY!
Directions: Connect the dots from 1 to 7 to find where Blue is sleeping. Color the picture.
60

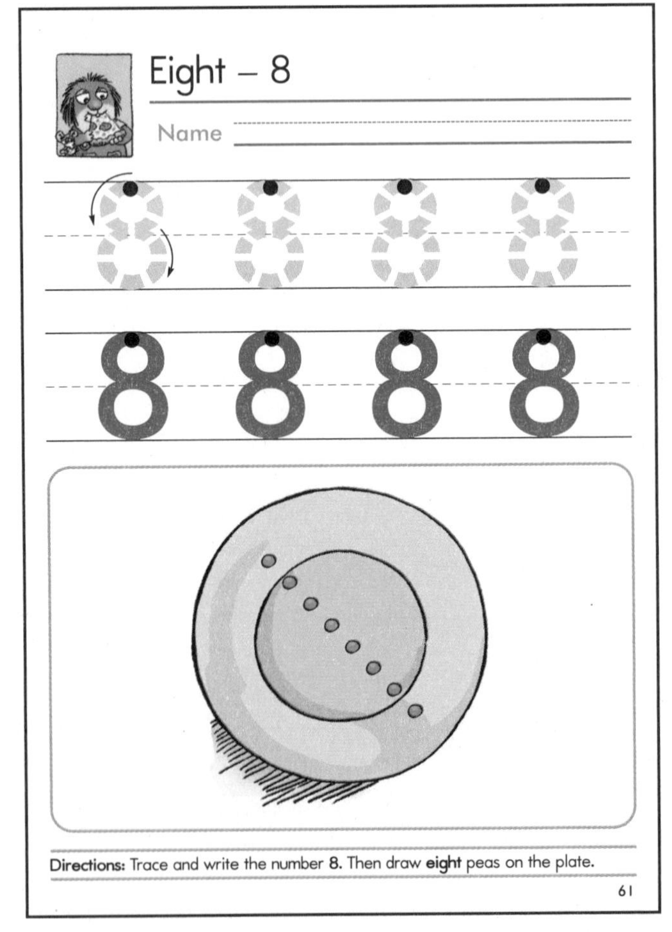
Eight – 8
Name
Directions: Trace and write the number 8. Then draw eight peas on the plate.
61

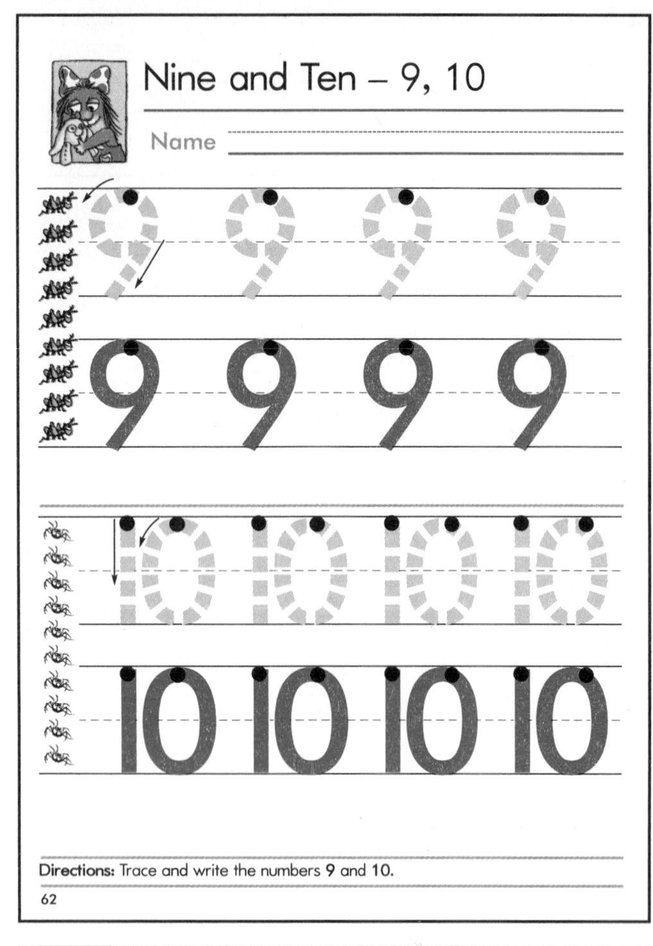
Nine and Ten – 9, 10
Name
9 9 9 9
10 10 10 10
Directions: Trace and write the numbers 9 and 10.
62

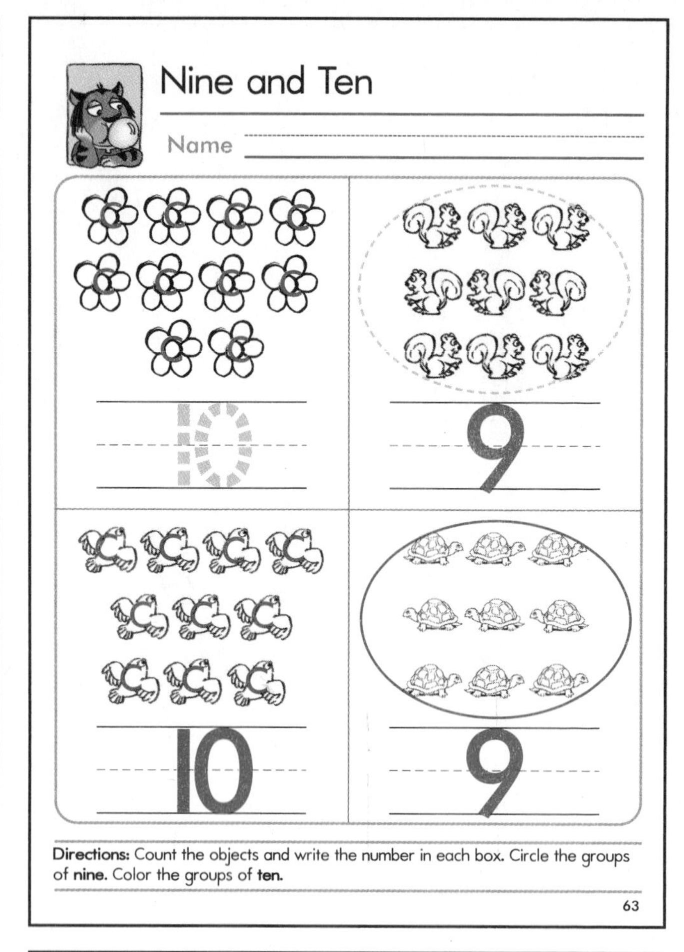
Nine and Ten
Name
10
9
10
9
Directions: Count the objects and write the number in each box. Circle the groups of nine. Color the groups of ten.
63

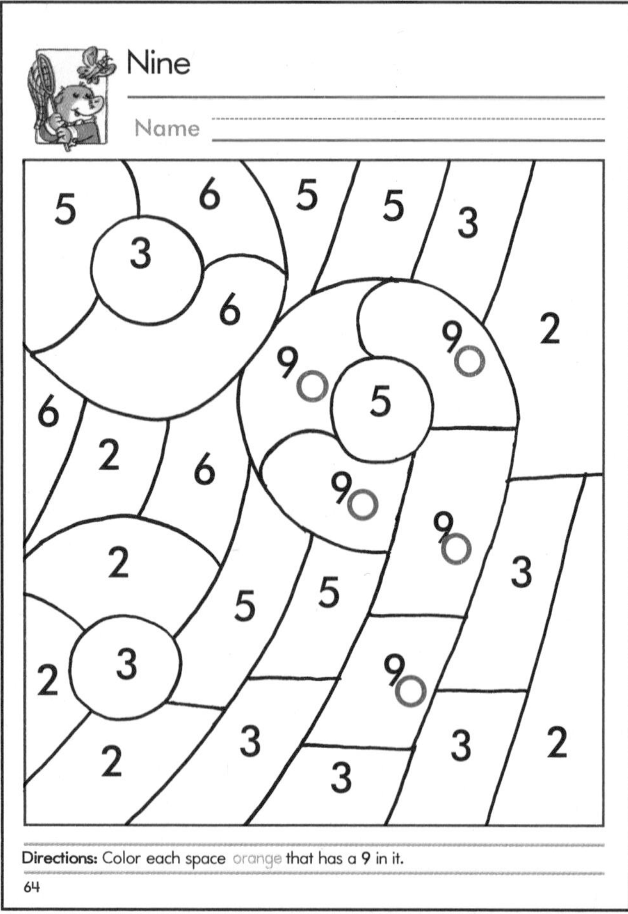
Nine
Name
Directions: Color each space orange that has a 9 in it.
64

Writing Your Telephone Number
Name
Answers will vary.
1 2 3
4 5 6
7 8 9
* 0 #
Directions: Have an adult write your phone number on the line above. Practice dialing it using the phone in the picture. Then color in the numbers of your phone number on the phone.
65

Numbers 1 to 10: Review

Name

Directions: Look at Little Sister's hopscotch board. Help her fill in the missing numbers.

66

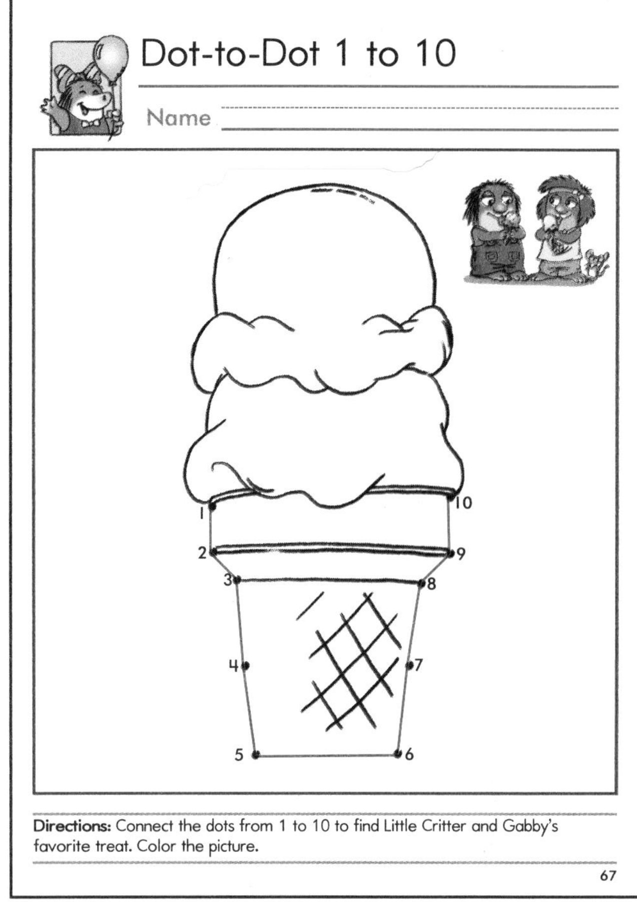

Dot-to-Dot 1 to 10

Name

Directions: Connect the dots from 1 to 10 to find Little Critter and Gabby's favorite treat. Color the picture.

67

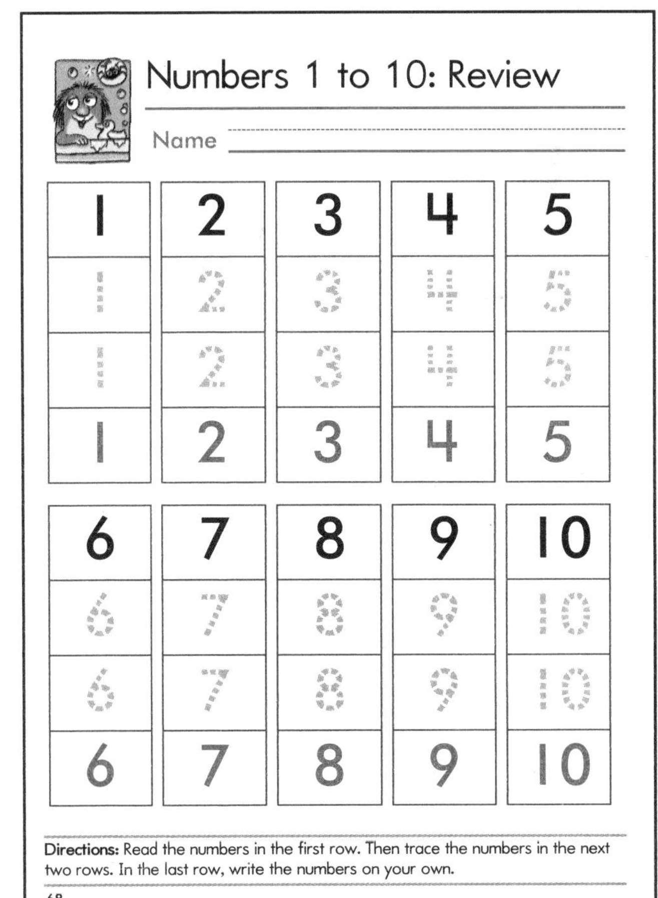

Numbers 1 to 10: Review

Name

1	2	3	4	5
1	2	3	4	5
1	2	3	4	5
1	2	3	4	5

6	7	8	9	10
6	7	8	9	10
6	7	8	9	10
6	7	8	9	10

Directions: Read the numbers in the first row. Then trace the numbers in the next two rows. In the last row, write the numbers on your own.

68

Number Matching

Name

Directions: Draw a line to the matching numbers.

69

Number Practice 1 to 20
Name
1 2
3 4 5
6 7 8
Answers will vary.
9 10 11
12 13 14
15 16 17
18 19 20
Directions: Say the name of each number as you trace it. How high can you count?
70

Dot-to-Dot 1 to 20
Name
Directions: Connect the dots from 1 to 20 to find what Little Critter builds at the beach. Color the picture.
71

What Comes Next?
Name
3, 4
5, 6
1, 2
4, 5
2, 3
6, 7
Directions: What comes next? Write the number on the line.
72

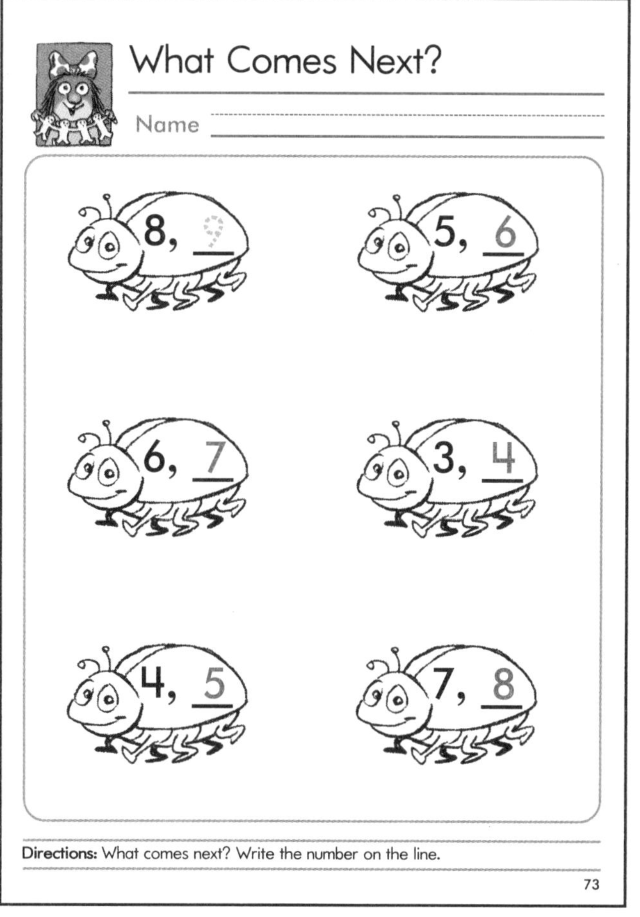
What Comes Next?
Name
8, 9
5, 6
6, 7
3, 4
4, 5
7, 8
Directions: What comes next? Write the number on the line.
73

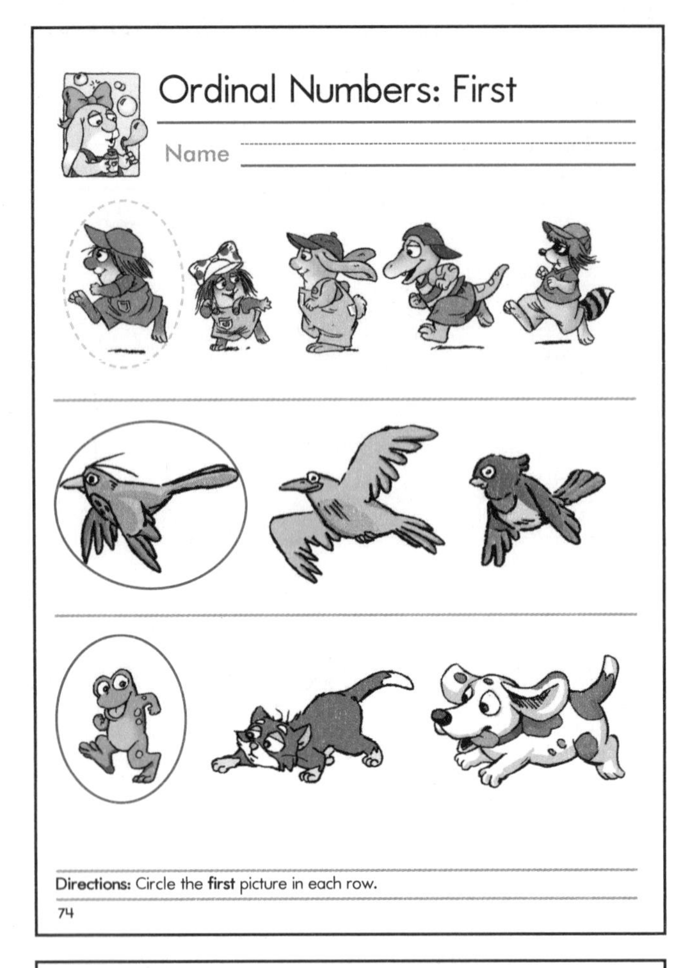

Ordinal Numbers: First

Name ______________________

Directions: Circle the **first** picture in each row.

74

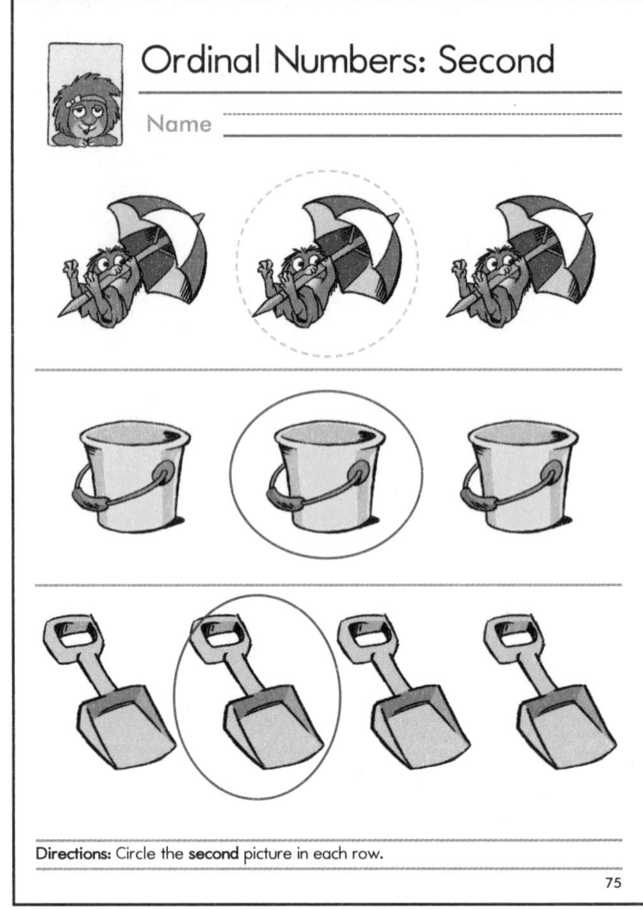

Ordinal Numbers: Second

Name ______________________

Directions: Circle the **second** picture in each row.

75

Ordinal Numbers: Third

Name ______________________

Directions: Circle the **third** picture in each row.

76

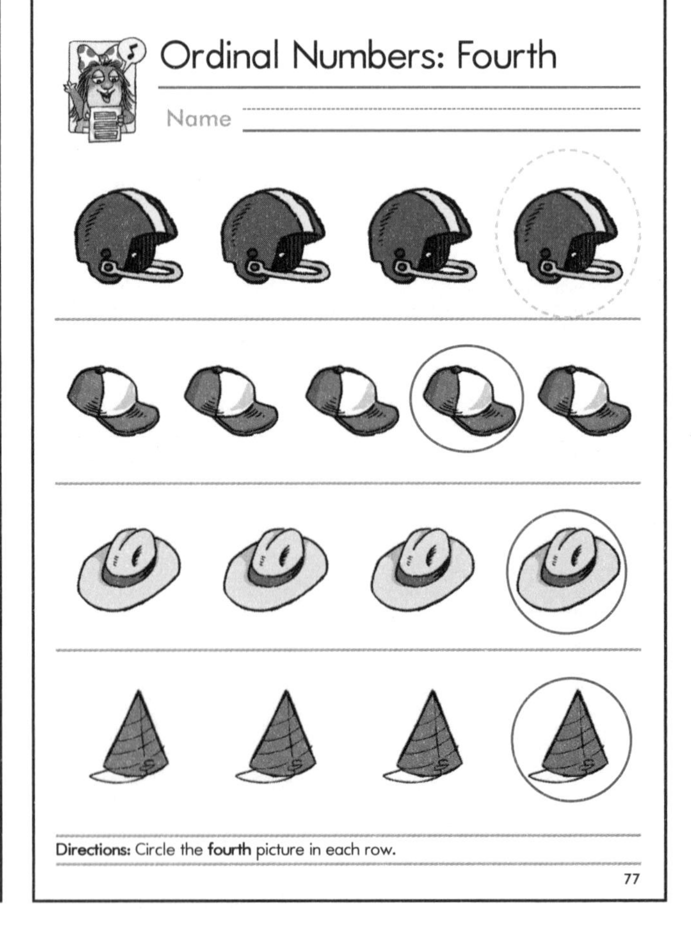

Ordinal Numbers: Fourth

Name ______________________

Directions: Circle the **fourth** picture in each row.

77

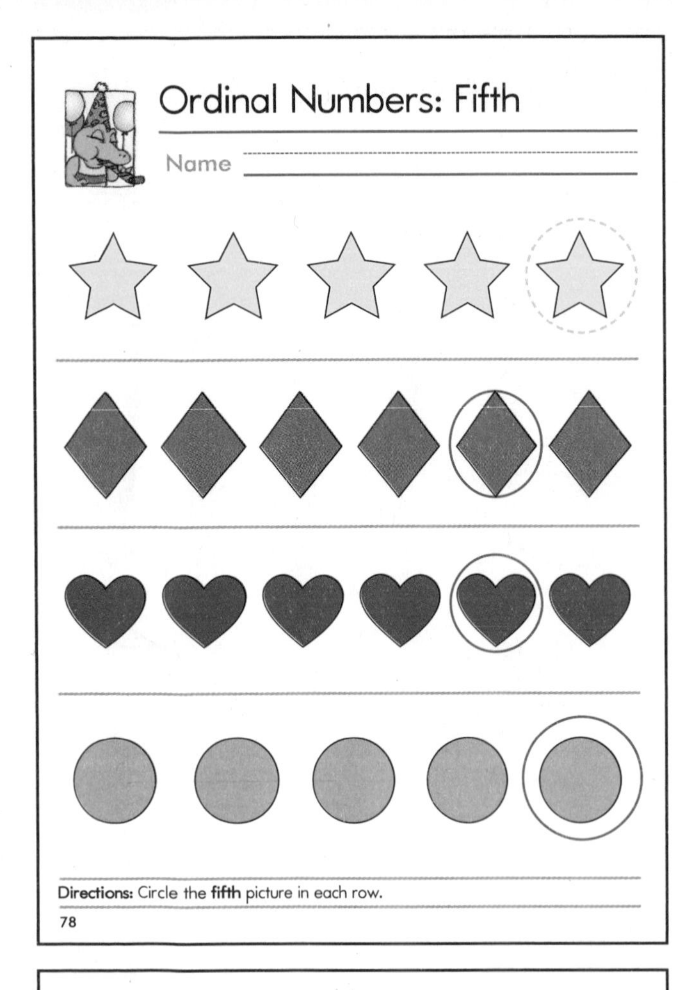

Ordinal Numbers: Fifth

Name

Directions: Circle the **fifth** picture in each row.

78

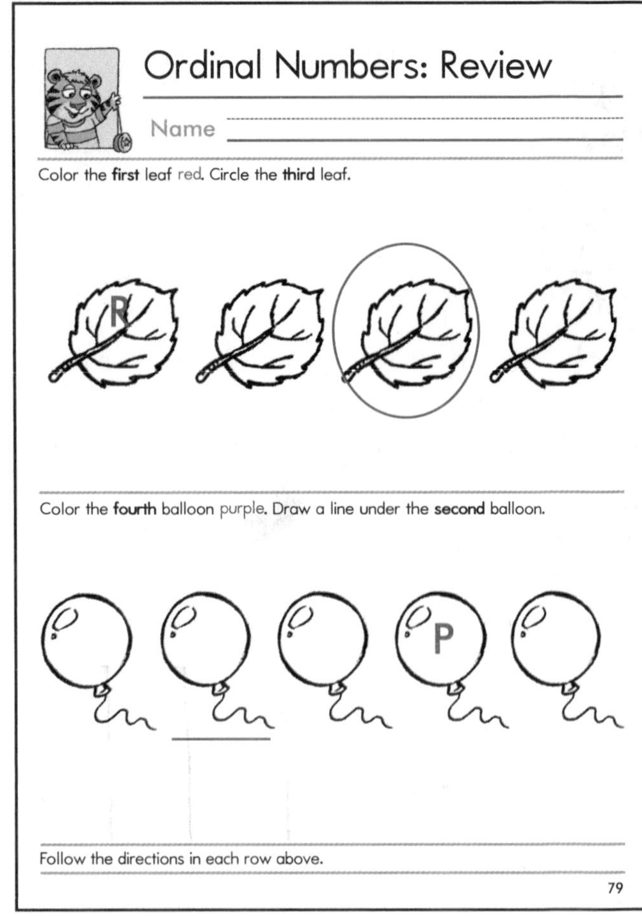

Ordinal Numbers: Review

Name

Color the **first** leaf red. Circle the **third** leaf.

Color the **fourth** balloon purple. Draw a line under the **second** balloon.

Follow the directions in each row above.

79

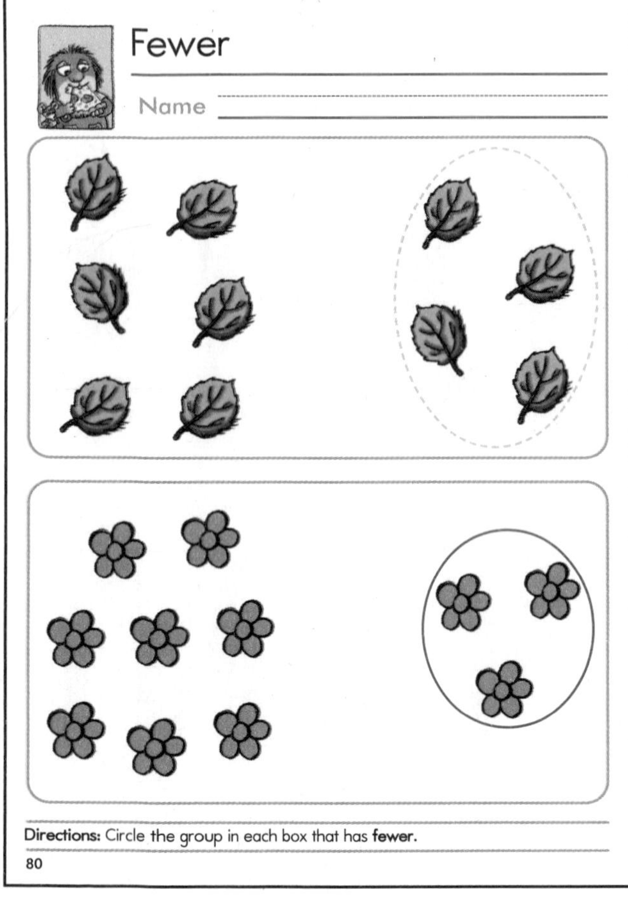

Fewer

Name

Directions: Circle the group in each box that has **fewer**.

80

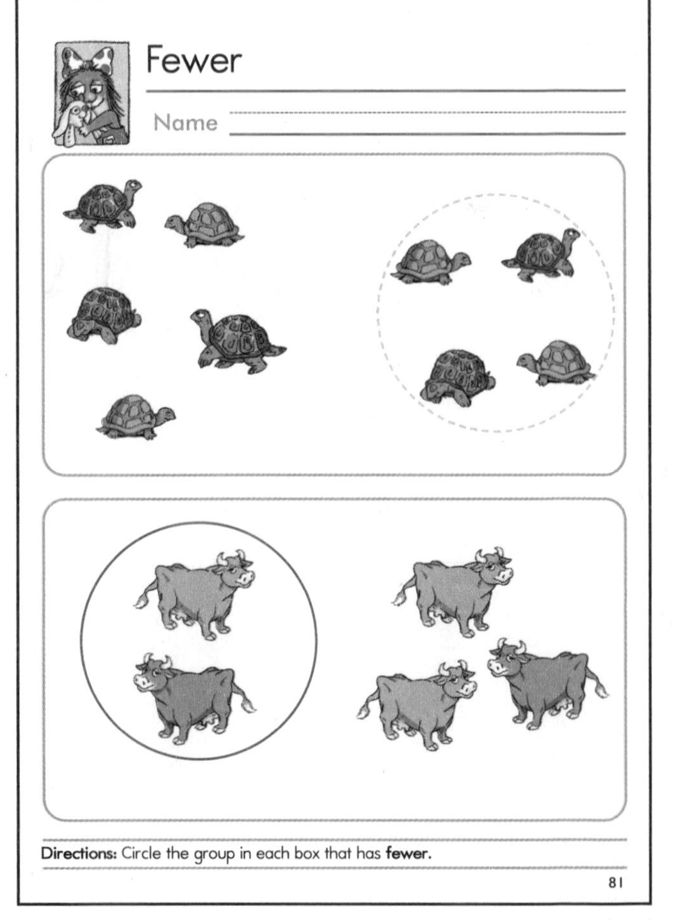

Fewer

Name

Directions: Circle the group in each box that has **fewer**.

81

Fewer

Name

Directions: Circle the group in each box that has **fewer.**

82

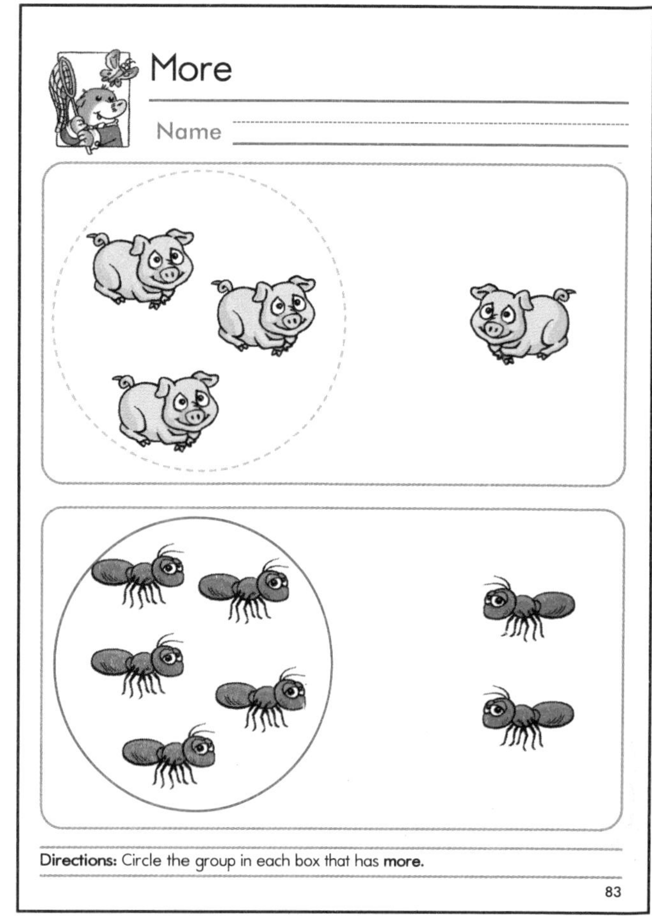

More

Name

Directions: Circle the group in each box that has **more.**

83

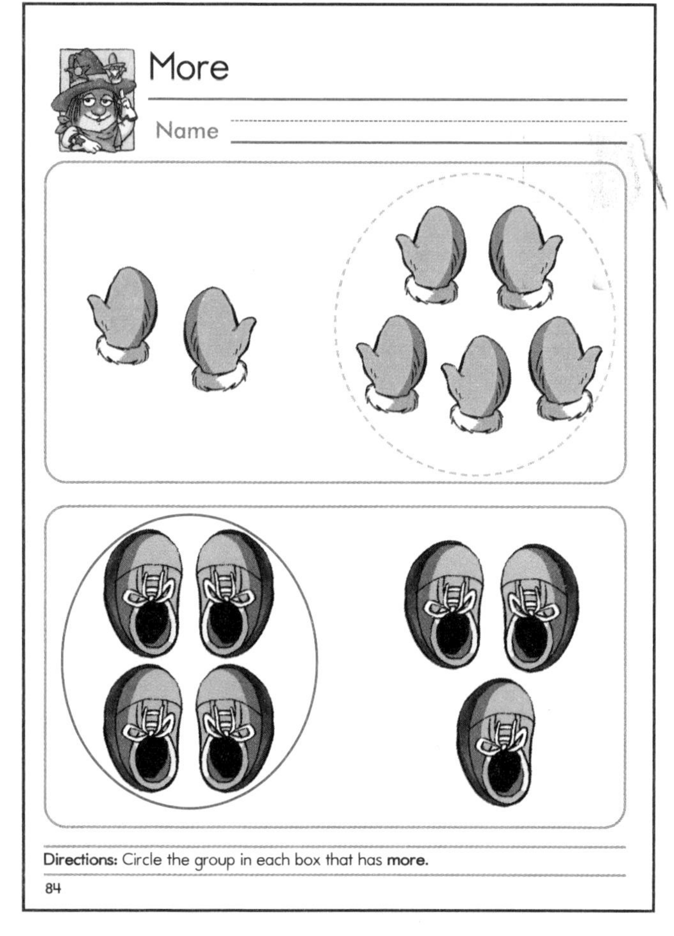

More

Name

Directions: Circle the group in each box that has **more.**

84

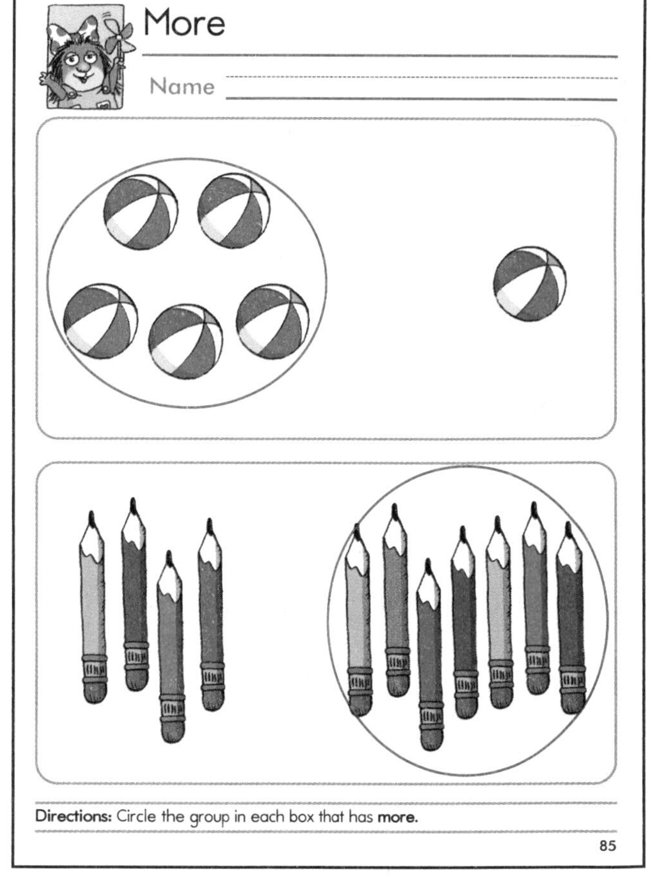

More

Name

Directions: Circle the group in each box that has **more.**

85

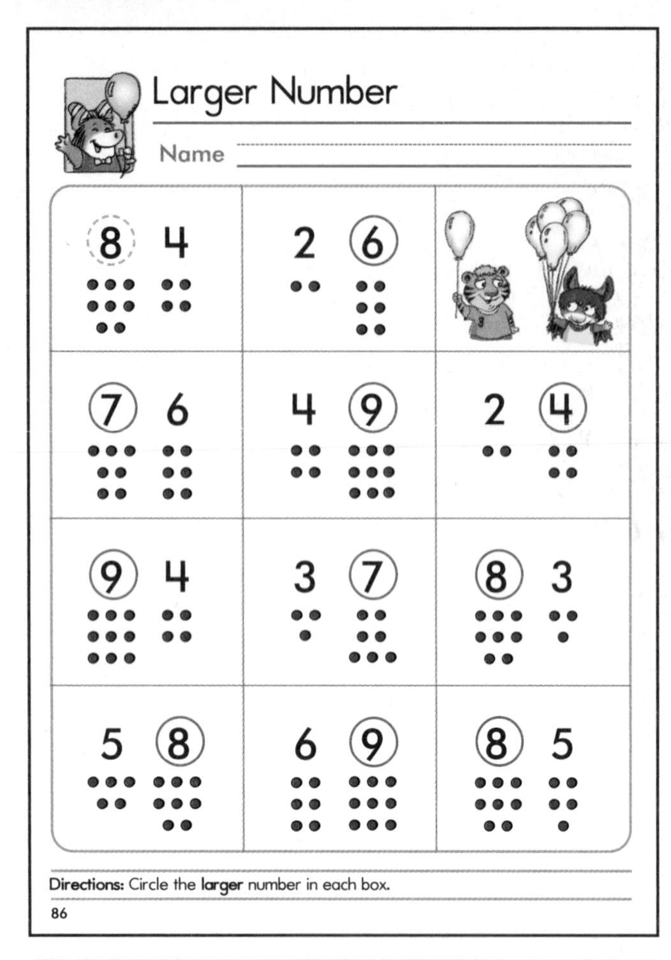

Larger Number

Name

8 4	2 6	
7 6	4 9	2 4
9 4	3 7	8 3
5 8	6 9	8 5

Directions: Circle the **larger** number in each box.

86

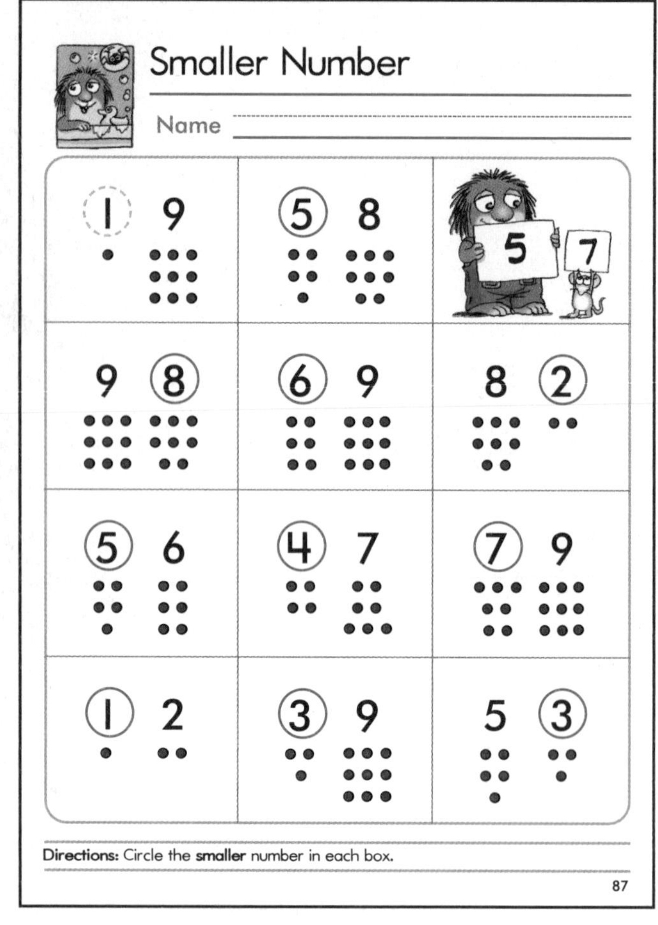

Smaller Number

Name

1 9	5 8	
9 8	6 9	8 2
5 6	4 7	7 9
1 2	3 9	5 3

Directions: Circle the **smaller** number in each box.

87

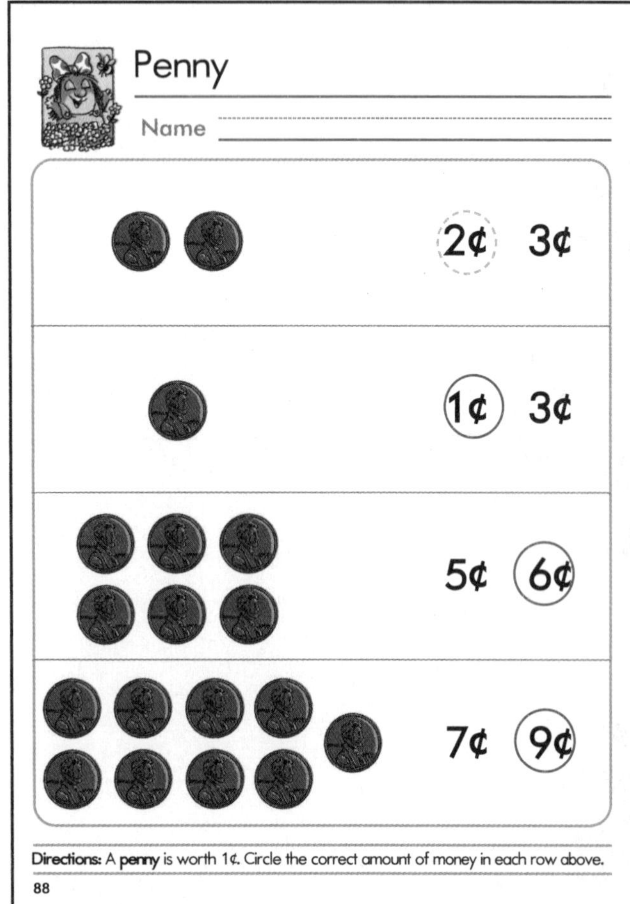

Penny

Name

2¢ 3¢

1¢ 3¢

5¢ 6¢

7¢ 9¢

Directions: A **penny** is worth 1¢. Circle the correct amount of money in each row above.

88

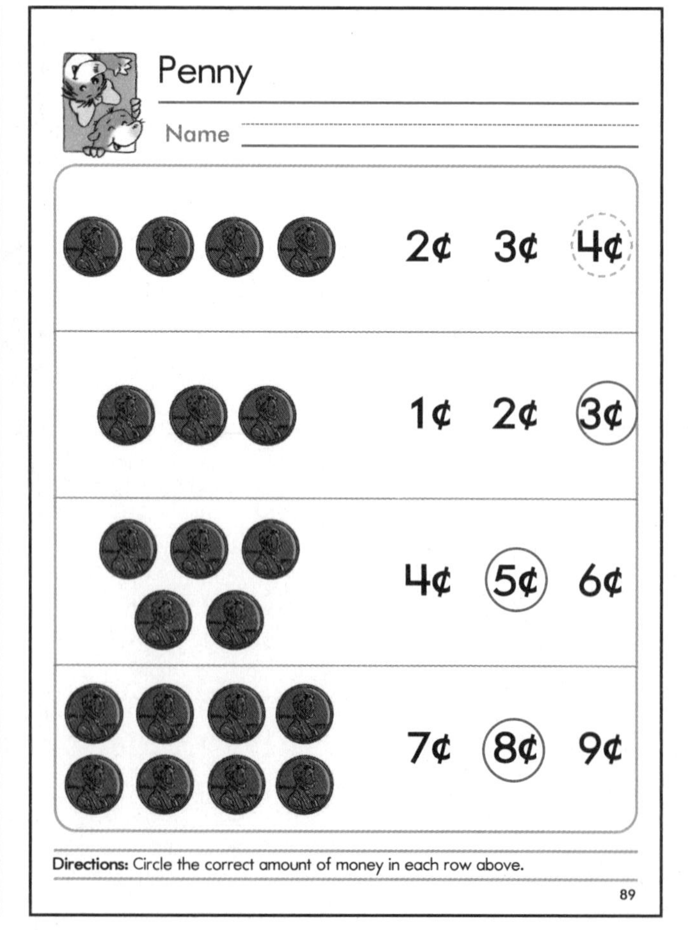

Penny

Name

2¢ 3¢ 4¢

1¢ 2¢ 3¢

4¢ 5¢ 6¢

7¢ 8¢ 9¢

Directions: Circle the correct amount of money in each row above.

89

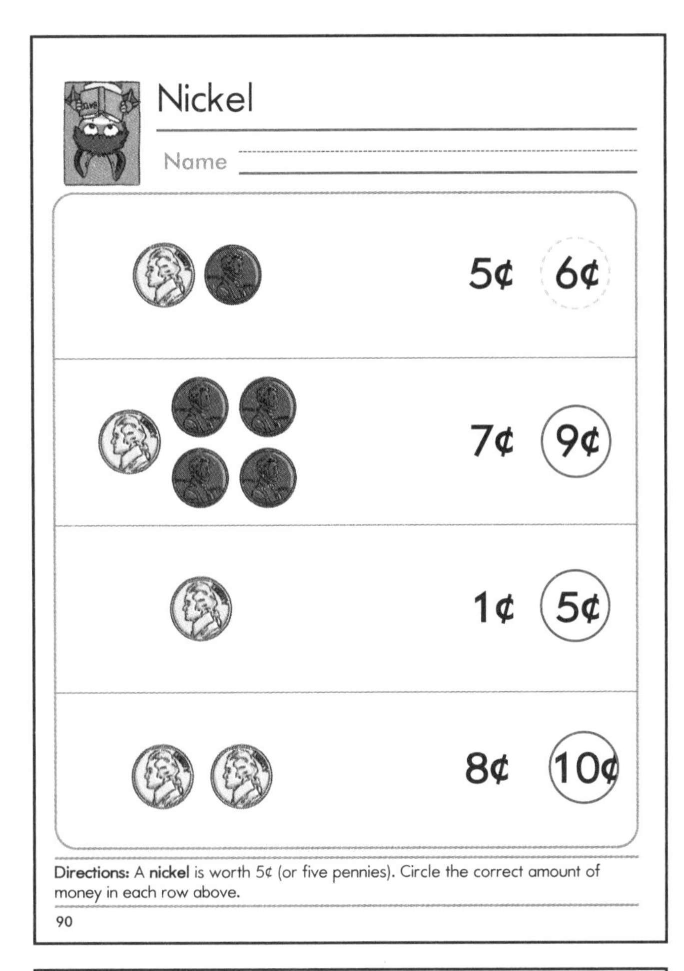
Nickel
Name
5¢ 6¢
7¢ 9¢
1¢ 5¢
8¢ 10¢
Directions: A nickel is worth 5¢ (or five pennies). Circle the correct amount of money in each row above.
90

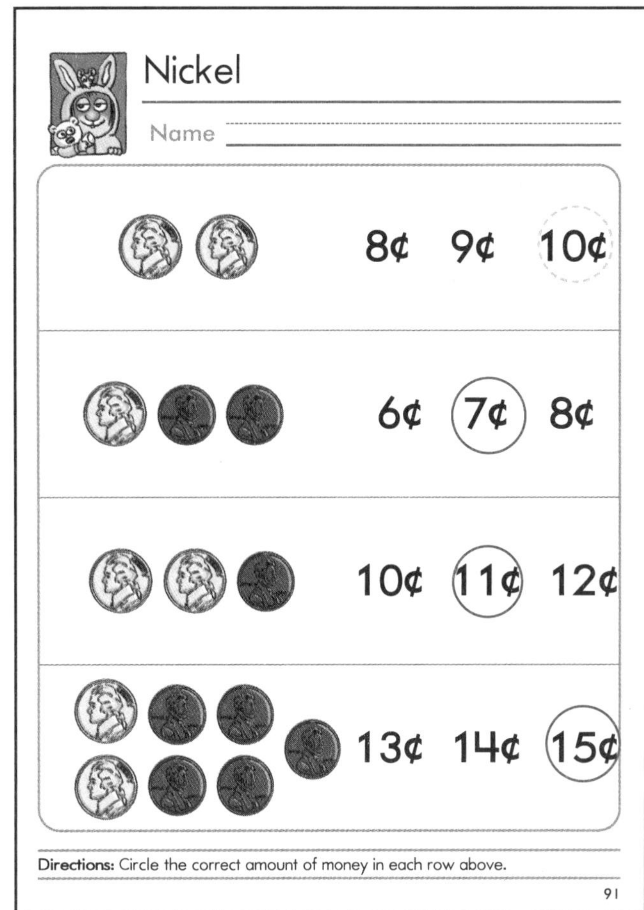
Nickel
Name
8¢ 9¢ 10¢
6¢ 7¢ 8¢
10¢ 11¢ 12¢
13¢ 14¢ 15¢
Directions: Circle the correct amount of money in each row above.
91

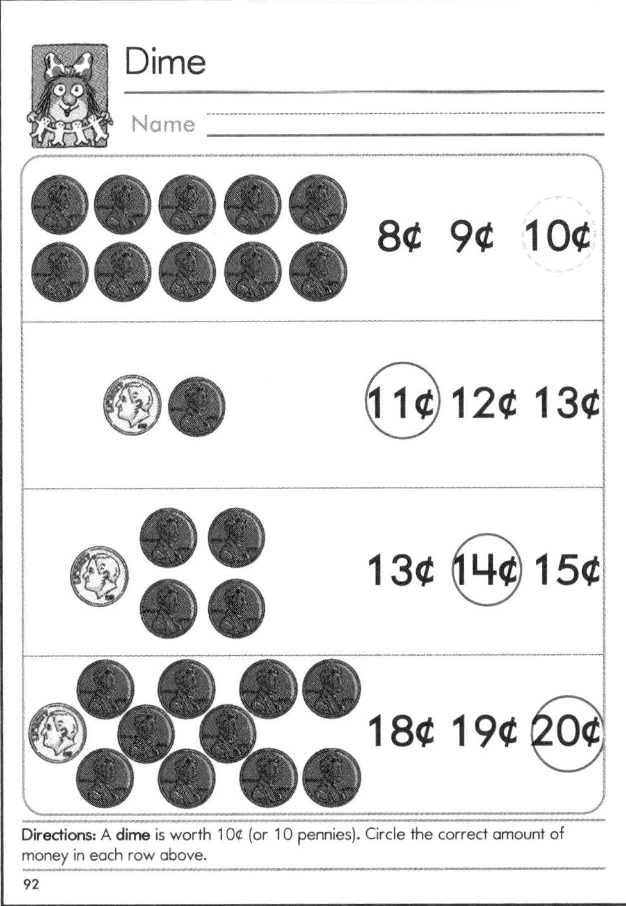
Dime
Name
8¢ 9¢ 10¢
11¢ 12¢ 13¢
13¢ 14¢ 15¢
18¢ 19¢ 20¢
Directions: A dime is worth 10¢ (or 10 pennies). Circle the correct amount of money in each row above.
92

Quarter
Name
25¢
25¢
10¢
25¢
25¢
10¢
25¢
25¢
5¢
25¢
5¢
10¢
Directions: A quarter is worth 25¢. Help Little Critter find all of the things that cost 25¢. Draw an X on each one.
93

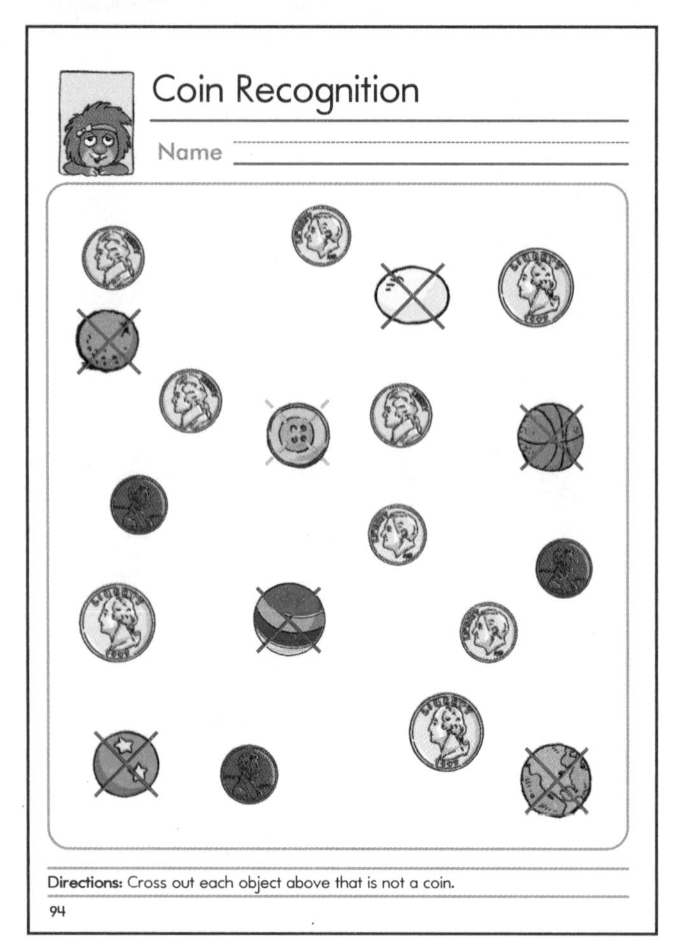

Coin Recognition

Name

Directions: Cross out each object above that is not a coin.

94

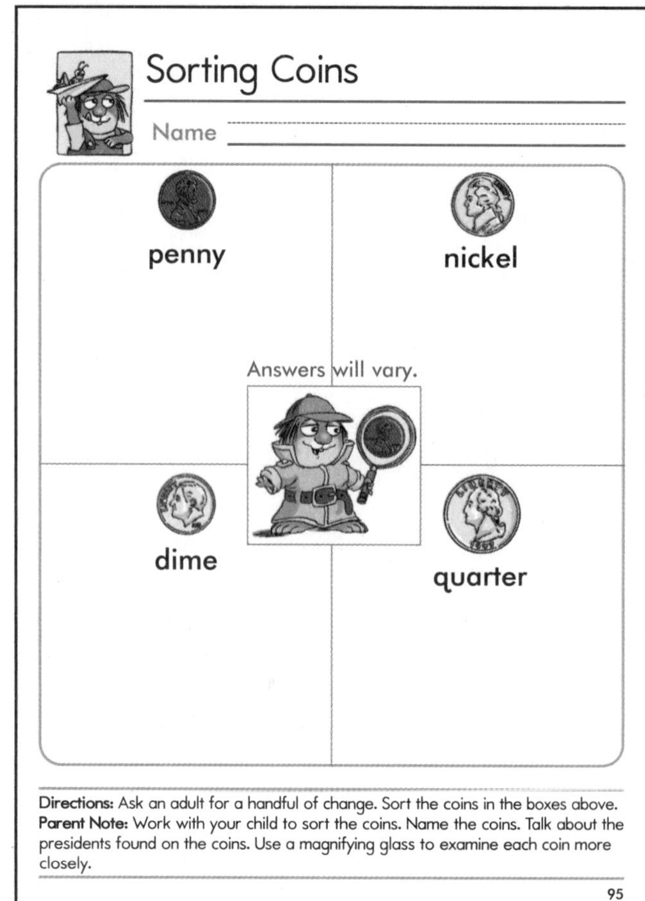

Sorting Coins

Name

penny

nickel

Answers will vary.

dime

quarter

Directions: Ask an adult for a handful of change. Sort the coins in the boxes above.
Parent Note: Work with your child to sort the coins. Name the coins. Talk about the presidents found on the coins. Use a magnifying glass to examine each coin more closely.

95

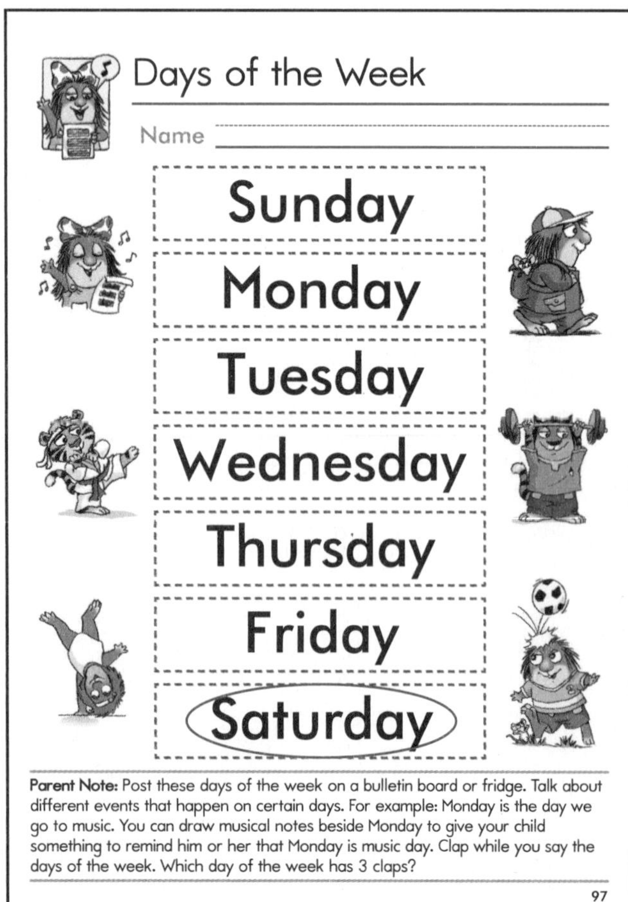

Days of the Week

Name

Sunday

Monday

Tuesday

Wednesday

Thursday

Friday

Saturday

Parent Note: Post these days of the week on a bulletin board or fridge. Talk about different events that happen on certain days. For example: Monday is the day we go to music. You can draw musical notes beside Monday to give your child something to remind him or her that Monday is music day. Clap while you say the days of the week. Which day of the week has 3 claps?

97

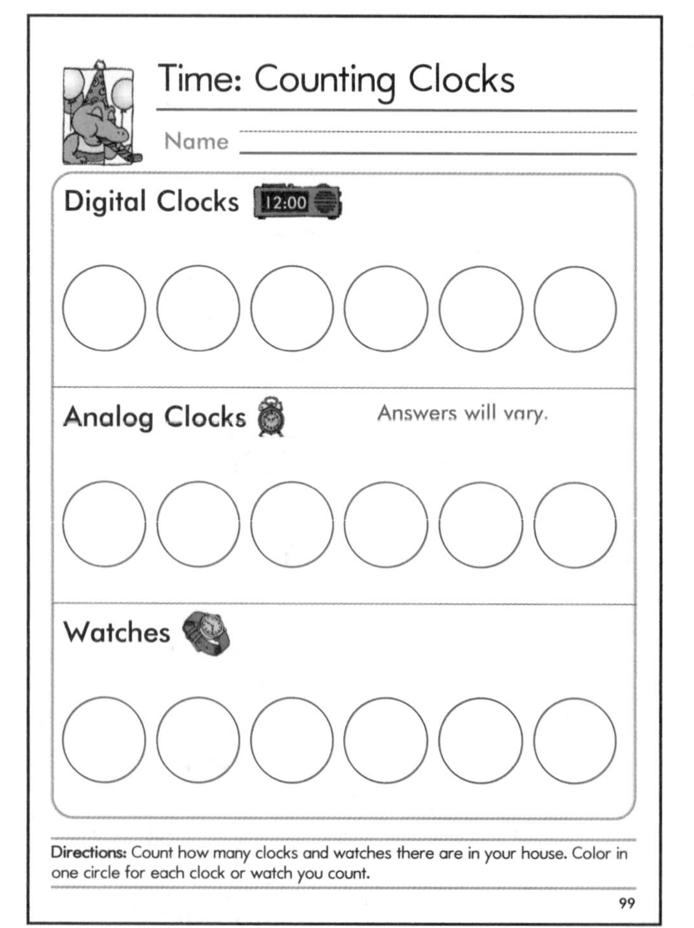

Time: Counting Clocks

Name

Digital Clocks

12:00

Analog Clocks

Answers will vary.

Watches

Directions: Count how many clocks and watches there are in your house. Color in one circle for each clock or watch you count.

99

Time: Numbers on the Clock

Name

Directions: Trace the numbers 1 to 12 in order on the clock.

100

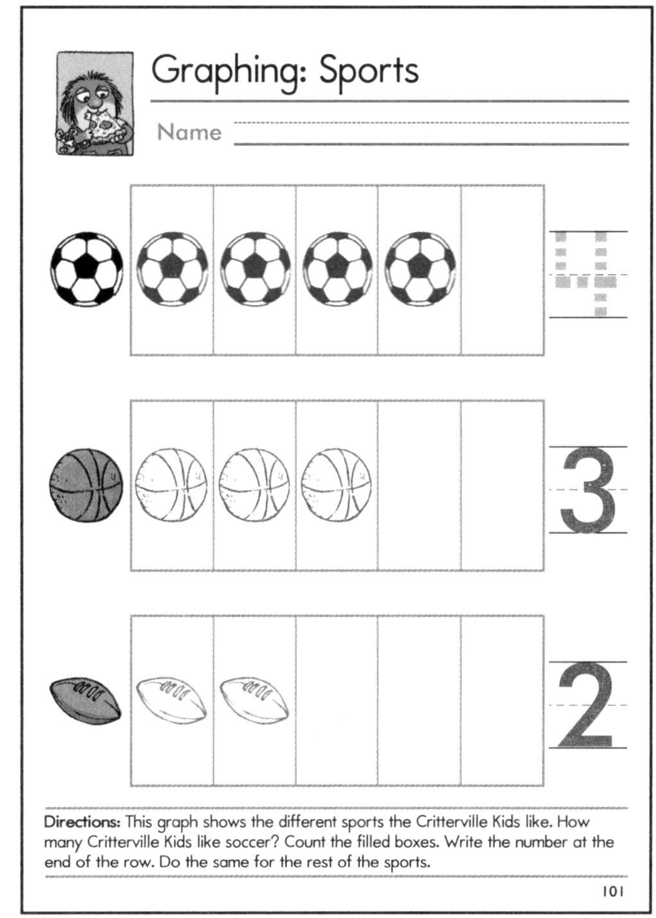

Graphing: Sports

Name

Directions: This graph shows the different sports the Critterville Kids like. How many Critterville Kids like soccer? Count the filled boxes. Write the number at the end of the row. Do the same for the rest of the sports.

101

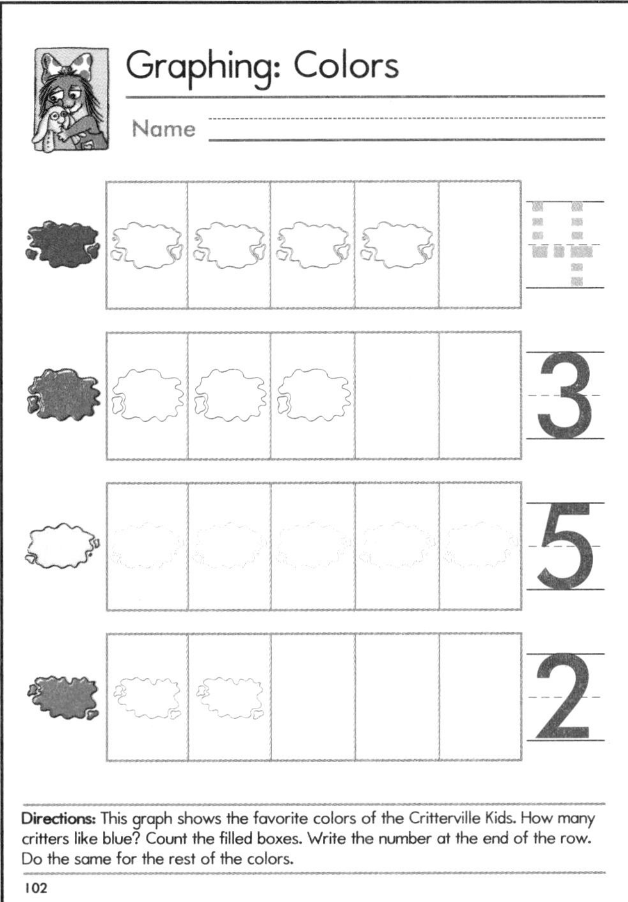

Graphing: Colors

Name

Directions: This graph shows the favorite colors of the Critterville Kids. How many critters like blue? Count the filled boxes. Write the number at the end of the row. Do the same for the rest of the colors.

102

Graphing: Pets

Name

Directions: Help Little Critter count the pets in the window. Then color one box for each animal on the graph above. The first one is done for you.

103

Graphing: Food

Name

★ How many critters like hot dogs best? 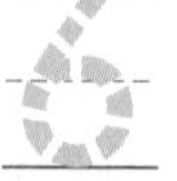

★ How many critters like pizza best? 

★ How many critters like chicken best? 6

★ Circle the food that most critters like best.

 hot dog

 hamburger

 pizza

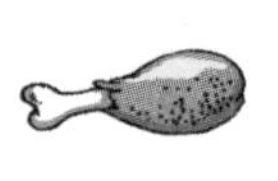 chicken

Directions: Have an adult read the questions above. Then answer the questions about the graph on page 104.

Sequencing: Little Sister

Name

1st

2nd

3rd

Directions: Have an adult carefully tear out page 107 and cut out the pictures. Then, arrange the pictures to show what happened 1st, 2nd, and 3rd. Glue the pictures on this page.

Sequencing: Dad

Name

1st

2nd

3rd

Directions: Have an adult carefully tear out page 109 and cut out the pictures. Then, arrange the pictures to show what happened 1st, 2nd, and 3rd. Glue the pictures on this page.

Sequencing: Gabby

Name

1st

2nd

3rd

Directions: Have an adult carefully tear out page 113 and cut out the pictures. Then, arrange the pictures to show what happened 1st, 2nd, and 3rd. Glue the pictures on this page.

Sequencing: Little Critter and Blue

Name

Directions: Write a number in each box to show the correct order in which to tell the story.

115

Sequencing: Snowcritter

Name

1st

2nd

3rd

Answers will vary.

4th

Directions: Have an adult carefully tear out page 117 and cut out the pictures. Then, arrange the pictures to show what happened 1st, 2nd, and 3rd. Draw your own picture to show what happened next. Finally, glue the pictures on this page.

116

Thinking Skills

Name

- The house is white.
- The house has a red door.
- The house has a fence in front of it.

Directions: Read the clues above. Draw an **X** on each house that does not fit the clues. Circle the correct house.

119

Thinking Skills

Name

- The mitten is green.
- The mitten has two different shapes on it.
- The mitten has hearts on it.

Directions: Read the clues above. Draw an **X** on each mitten that does not fit the clues. Circle the correct mitten.

120

NOTES

NOTES